Emerging Downunder

Ray Simpson
with
Brent Lyons Lee

Emerging Downunder, provides an intriguing book at the merging church from the viewpoint of Celtic spirituality. It challenges us to believe that Celtic wisdom provides a framework in which to re imagine the church downunder with the hope of healing for both our land and our peoples. The earthiness of Celtic spirituality with its love of the land, its concern for hospitality and prayer will resonate with many Australians who are searching for a way to connect their faith to every part of there lives. This is an important and timely book.

Christine and Tom Sine
Mustard Seed Associates

This is such an insightful book on the emerging spirituality and Christian expression of the search for meaning, integrity and authenticity. The authors have creatively articulated the tickling of the spirit that so many people experience that there is more than what we have experienced so far. The world and both Australia and New Zealand are changing. What this book creates is an exploration of the mystery that surrounds the merging realities. Perhaps most of all it engenders a sense of hope. Hope that the living Spirit of God is integrating faith and culture, context and realities. It is an important read and even more important vision of some helpful signposts.

Fuzz Kitto
Spirited Consulting
Converse Emerging Church Network

Emerging Downunder

Creating New Monastic Villages of God

Ray Simpson
with Brent Lyons Lee

ATF Press
Adelaide

First published 2008
Reprinted 2016

ISBN 978 1920 691 912   Paperback
      978 1925 486 063   Hardback
      978 1925 486 070   ePub
      978 1925 486 087   pdf

Cover design: painting by Kelly Scott used with permission (contact Urban Seed in Melbourne for details). Cover design by Astrid Sengkey.

ATF Press
An imprint of the Australasian Theological Forum Ltd
P O Box 504
Hindmarsh
SA 5007
ABN 90 116 359 963
www.atfpress.com

Contents

Foreword   vii

Introduction   ix

1. Ray's Reflections on Australia   3

2. What is Dying?   17

3. What is Being Born Again?   29

4. Needed Features for Emerging Churches   45

5. Fresh Shoots Downunder   79

6. New Monasticism   119

Epilogue: Lands of the Eternal Spirit   133

End Notes   143

Index   147

Foreword

The pages you are about to read are full of rich insight and wisdom. Don't start reading if you are happy with the status quo—if you feel your life is well balanced, or that your church is a happy, harmonious, well-oiled machine—these pages simply won't work for you.

This is a read for the restless; those who are hungry for something deeper, who cringe with what passes for Christian identity and worship these days and despair when they read church pew bulletins. In fact many who now feel church-less may well find hope here. Or those who walk a lonely path of spiritual isolation where soul mates are rare.

Ray Simpson brings the depth of his experience in Celtic tradition based in The Community of Aidan and Hilda in the UK which gives an insightful overview of the challenges facing the church in Australia and New Zealand. He weaves the impressions he received from his time here where he listened, read and observed widely with the depth of his study and background in the centuries-old tradition known as the Celtic spirituality. Brent Lyons Lee has initiated this conversation in order to better serve in the emerging church here in Australia.

There are some huge challenges in these humble pages, such as: 'We are called to cradle a Christian spirituality for today that brings healing to our lands' and 'Australia has an opportunity to birth something in the third millennium which can give hope to the declining old world and to the nascent new world.'

In order to respond to these challenges the shape of the emerging church is explored through the window of Celtic wisdom. At its heart is humility, earthiness, a relinquishment of power and formality and an openness to fresh ways of embracing home, hospitality and a prayerful connectedness to God.

I think it is a timely book. These days I am not in formal ministry in a church as I lead World Vision Australia but I am often speaking in churches or in Christian contexts. I am struck by a sad uniformity of styles, expressions, even songs. I cringe with the clichés that pass as being meaningful ways of worship. And I often leave these churches asking—what is it all about? I do not think I am alone. We live in complex times and the church is caught up in a culture full of a cacophony of competing influences. It takes wisdom and insight to look at it afresh so I commend this book as a thoughtful, challenging and instructive means of listening to the winds of the Spirit for a way to emerge into the future.

Tim Costello
December 2007

Introduction

Brent's thoughts:

At age twenty-nine, I'm apparently an 'emerging church' leader. The 'emerging church' term has been used to describe a fresh paradigm for church. I think the term has by default described doing 'worship' in new and 'cool' ways. Some parts of the emerging movement have included the idea of being 'missional' which has often lead to groups not taking time for worship at all. I came across a book not long ago written in 1970 entitled 'Emerging Church'. To be reminded that this concept is not new was quite refreshing—every generation needs to look for 'new' ways of doing and being church. I point this out not to undermine the momentum created by the emerging church dialogue, but to give some perspective. We the Church have managed to survive for two thousand years!

In thinking about a title for this book, it was almost more appropriate to use the term 'submerging' rather than 'emerging'. David Tacey writes that in contemporary post-colonial Australia, spirituality is entering our life from below, and the feet play a more important role than the intellect. He quotes Barbara Blackman as saying that if we want to 'understand' spirituality in this country we have to 'stand-under' our habitual logic and our usual perceptions, since that is the vantage point from which the spirit is found. Understanding calls us away from our conscious conventions.[1]

Heritage

I'm Anglo-Celtic through and through; Scottish on my maternal side, English and Irish on my paternal side. I'm at least a third generation Aussie. I think I feel more comfortable with the angst of Gen X even though I'm technically Gen Y. When I speak publicly I often apologise up front about being Gen Y, but will joke that I'm not a good one because I've worked with the same organisation for several years and I have moved out of home and married! A lot is made of generational differences. One thing that is certain for people of my generation (and for all generations) is that the world is different and there is seemingly no certainty. Foundations that have been satisfactory in the past have been questioned to the point of being meaningless—even church.

Like many others, I found myself looking for meaning in the concrete act of tracing the footsteps of my ancestors. In 2004, my wife and I travelled to the UK. It was a holiday; but more important for us was to tread in the places our ancestors had trodden. We also wanted to explore our growing interest in Celtic spirituality. The holiday was great. Going to Royal Tunbridge Wells, where parts of my family originated, was amazing. However the greatest experience was the sense that the fingerprints of generations of people, some of who I may have been related to, were everywhere.

We made a number of pilgrimages to 'holy' sites around Europe, from the tiny monastic village of Glendalough in Ireland to the massive St Peters Basilica in Rome. Most transforming was a little tidal island off the east coast of Northumbria called Lindisfarne, or Holy Island. There we met Ray Simpson who lived on the island as the Guardian of the Community of Aidan and Hilda. There was an instant connection as fellow lifelong learners. I was drawn to Ray as I consider him a mystic. I'm quite intuitive, but I'm much more a pragmatist, yet I felt God on that island like never before. I experienced what the Celts call the 'thin places'—where only a thin veil exists between the material and spiritual.

Beyond the isolation of Holy Island, even in the bustle of tourist filled cathedrals, something was very different. I became aware of my own sense of mortality as I visited such historical sites, getting some perspective on the slice of time each person is allotted. Life viewed from the perspective of death is indeed an important component of Christian discipleship, one which we shy away from—the unknown is scary!

Returning to Australia

I came back to Australia after only several weeks away and felt like an exile in what I had always thought of as 'my' country. I wasn't sure how to make sense of my experience. The Australian psyche seemed best described as a teenager with no life experience, motoring on with the attitude of invincibility found in youth, compounded by its unwillingness to reflect on mistakes and learn from them. And it's true; Australia is a young country with a lot of growing up to do.

Reading David Tacey (who I regard as a most insightful author on Australian Spirituality) hit the mark for me. Tacey writes that the power of the land and the influence of aboriginal culture are activating primordial levels of the Euro-Australian psyche, stirring its deeper layers. He believes that a version of ancient Celtic spirituality is being awakened and stirred to new life in Australia. One can see this in many different ways in Australian folk culture, where the attempt to 'grow down' into Australian soil has the effect of revitalising Celtic roots, giving rise to a kind of Celtic revival.[2]

Indigenous people in Australia find their identity through the connection with their land. I never really knew what that meant until I went to the UK and started walking on the land of my ancestors and hearing the stories of 'my' people. I began to gain some perspective on the importance of the land to indig-enous people, it's something that is intuitive and too hard to describe rationally.

I desperately wanted to be back in the UK where it seemed like there was a bit of perspective. I found myself hungry to name and locate an authentic Australian spirituality. Anglo-Australian history is not much more than two hundred years old, yet Indigenous Australian history dates back as far as mythology can recall. I needed to tap in to this spirit, into this dreaming, but didn't feel like I had the right. So I shared my thoughts with a local Indigenous man. He looked me stead-fastly in the eyes and simply said: 'This is your place'. Being given permission to believe this was my place changed every-thing. Even though he and I weren't the individuals killing each other a few hundred years ago, there was a real acknow-ledgment that we, the ancestors, could struggle forward.

Under ten years of John Howard we may have given up on the hope of an official apology for the atrocities inflicted by Europeans on Indigenous Australians. Yet while our govern-ment is not changing its mind, the reality is that every generation is going to have to say sorry. In every generation to come, Indigenous and non-indigenous Australians will have to look each other in the eyes and ask: 'Where to from here?' Having recently spent time in New Zealand, I believe Australians could learn a lot from our cousins about recon-ciliation. We will explore this later.

Inviting Ray

From all the emerging church and missional church literature, I found Ray Simpson's ideas on reconstructing ways forward for the people of God most compelling. In 2005, I invited Ray to come to Australia and discuss his Celtic spirituality insights. Following his visit, we have collaborated on applying his ideas in the unique 'Downunder' context. It is important to remember that there is nothing new under the sun. Yet these Celtic insights are drawn from ancient wisdom, and as we face the death of Christendom, I believe the time is right for them to re-emerge.

Ray's thoughts:

A bishop told me when I was twenty-nine that God had called me to have one foot in the church and one foot in the world outside. When Brent invited me Downunder I sought to come with a fresh eye, to see if I could discern as an outside friend any 'God insights'. Some of this book is a record of my encounters and reflections.

I serve a worldwide task force of Christians who seek to restore Christianity as a way of life. We have a few members and friends in New Zealand, as well as Australia, and church leaders from both countries spend time at 'The Open Gate', our Retreat House on England's Holy Island of Lindisfarne. So the reflections embrace both the Anzac countries.

I observed a new wave of spirituality in Australia, but it threatens to bypass the churches and leave them beached. So I thank God that there are some far-sighted Christians who see that a humbled church can tap into this new wave, and also into what is of God in the pre-European Aboriginal spirituality, so that a truly Australian and transforming church can rise up.

The Community of Aidan and Hilda is an international pilgrim people who seek to reconnect us with the Spirit and the scriptures, the streets and the soil, the saints and the seasons. Its members follow a Way of Life based on a rhythm of prayer, study, re-creation, simplicity, earth care and mission.

We are called to cradle a Christian spirituality for today that brings healing to our lands.

Australia has an opportunity to birth something in the third millennium which can give hope to the declining old world and to the nascent new world.

Columba of Iona left behind his 'old world' of Ireland and set foot in the 'new world' of the Scots in Britain. Two footprints carved in a rock on the Mull of Kintyre mark this spot. As I placed my feet in these prints, God's Spirit moved me to pray:

> May our friends Downunder be given
> the wild strength
> the bold faith
> the big heart
> the well stored mind
> the prophetic insight
> the inspired servant leadership
> and the missionary strategy
> of Columba.

From Columba's Iona Aidan, with gentle heart but backbone of steel, brought the torch of faith to the English speaking pagans and the original Britons, even though he was of another race. He set their hearts on fire. The faith became indigenous, drawing on the wisdom of the ancient peoples. Previous attempts to establish churches which were not truly indigenous lacked staying and drawing power.

Soon a deep transfiguration took place and the church of the English had its own birthright. This was enshrined in The Lindisfarne Gospels, whose non-routine illuminations, made in consultation with other major English monastic churches, form a kind of manifesto. The three highlights are:

- The Beatitudes (simplicity)
- The prodigal son (hospitality)
- Jesus' desert struggles (spiritual fitness)

Now it is Australia's turn to raise up athletes of the Spirit who will:

Re-kindle the fire
Draw from the ancient wells
Develop God-given rhythms
Establish compassionate communities
Heal the land
Transform the world.

Chapter 1

Ray's Reflections on Australia

Our first Community of Aidan and Hilda member in Australia was heavy metal band leader Brad Bessell, who phoned me after reading my first book *Exploring Celtic Spirituality: Historic Roots for Our Future* (Hodder and Stoughton). 'How do I plant a Celtic church?' he asked. I met many of Brad's friends in Adelaide who want authentic Christian spirituality but who have given up on anachronistic forms of church.

Brad wrote to me:

> Under our South Australian desert is the great artesian basin filled with millions of litres of water. The same could be said about the soul of this nation. It seems that church here looks for its nourishment from the seasonal rains that blow in from other countries. It comes and it goes and the land (church) is dry again. I believe that the Celtic Spirituality is not a seasonal rain or trend but something that is deeply buried under the Australian soul like our artesian waters under the desert. It is in the blood of the Scottish, Irish, Welsh, English convicts and immigrants. It just needs to be tapped. I believe that the role of Celtic Spirituality in this nation is to bring healing and reconciliation between

the Aboriginal and Non-Aboriginal. In fact, I
believe that had Celtic monks come to Australia
instead of convicts etc then the Aboriginal
people would have had a spiritual experience
similar to that of the ancient Celtic Christian. I
also believe the role of the Celtic renewal in this
nation is to encourage the Church to embrace a
faith that is more gentle and incarnational than
the colonial one that we have inherited from our
English forebears and less 'salesman' like than
the recent American models that we seem to
have embraced.

The second member of the Community I met is Matthew
Lamont, who lives in Newcastle, New South Wales. He had
completed a 'strong-man' competition in Perth and flew to
Britain's two holy islands of Lindisfarne and Iona. We met on
both islands. I liked his strength, but I liked something else
even more. This was a humility that recognised that there are
things of the spirit as well as of the body to be embraced. When
we met up in again in Sydney he was a different man. 'I
realised I had a choice between strength and wisdom', he told
me, 'I chose wisdom'. This reminded me of a story that Iona's
Saint Columba asked Christ to give him three gifts: prophecy,
purity and wisdom.

Matt told me that while he was on a day-long pilgrimage
around Iona, that he encountered God through stones he found.
He chose a stone that looked like a tear. He shed tears for the
baggage he had to leave behind. He took with him another
stone, shaped like a heart, which represented the compassion
which hitherto he had blocked. Back in Australia, he realised
that he was a sixth generation Australian, and it was time to

journey—not back to his forebears homes, but inwards to the heart of his own land.

As he recalled childhood visits to Boyagin Rock he intuited that this place is in some way sacred, and that he should re-visit it. Matt learned that long ago, when the Aboriginals had learned to live in harmony with each other and their environment, travel routes were opened up and there was more contact between the tribes. One day the Waugal, one of the mythological incarnations the Creator, presented himself in a dream to Buerma, a true-hearted tribesman, at a time when his tribe had lost contact with their laws and kinship. In the dream the earth was flooded and the tribe drowned, but the Waugal swam to safety, carrying those tribes-people who remained faithful to their traditions, until eventually they reached a sacred rock. This rock was Boyagin. Matt's experience did not mean that he had to adopt ancient tribal customs; it meant that he was to become aware of the divine and mysterious forces at work in the collective unconscious, then and now.

The ebbing tide of the imported and franchise models of church

I realised that Australia's churches, like its population, perch around the edge of the vast sub-continent, and tend to look back across the sea to Europe. Many of Britain's declining churches now realise that that, in their nineteenth-century form, they have reached the end of their shelf life. Rowan Williams the first Celtic Archbishop of Canterbury, calls on the inherited church to invest in entrepreneurial fresh expressions. Australia's churches are mostly imports from Europe, especially its Anglican and Baptist churches from England, its Presbyterian (and now Uniting) Churches from Scotland, and its Roman Catholic Churches from Ireland.

In other lands these churches have moved on, but Australia's churches seem more locked into their past. Adolescents become confident to launch out when they are secure in their roots. Are Australia's churches fearful of moving on because they clutch at these imported nineteenth-century models rather than find their own roots in the universal church and the soil of the southern cone?

Churches that stay in a rut end up as grave yards. I was not therefore surprised to find in bookshops Caroline Miley's *The Suicidal Church: Can the Anglican Church be Saved*? (Pluto Press). She claims that the Anglican Church in Australia has become a cultural ghetto of English middle-class Australians that provides no place for cross-cultural exchange. She does not mince her words. It is, she says, amateur, mediocre, hidebound by a bureaucratic way of decision-making which encourages dependency upon the hierarchy. Miley tells how Virginia Curran Hoffman applied to the church the principles of the Twelve Steps used by recovering alcoholics. Hoffman concludes that patterns of co-dependency and refusal to talk about feelings are more firmly entrenched in the church.

The imported model of church is second hand. It does not connect with the emerging Anzac society. I observed that one alternative to this is the franchise model. This comes from the USA. The message is 'You can do it yourselves, but you do it our way'. Various new churches follow prescribed 'menus' that are thought to guarantee 'success'. Most of this model comes from the American 'frontier' revivalist days. While we may thank God for all that is of the Spirit in these new churches, we also have a responsibility to ask serious questions. Does not a truly authentic church reflect in a hundred different ways the distinctive culture of the locality in which it is set, and of the way God's Spirit uniquely inter-acts with its people? Does not a holistic church draw deeply from more than one source?

The rising tide of spirituality

In between the Boxing Day Cricket and beach activities, I met David Tacey, whose spirituality classes at La Trobe University are often packed. I had read his *Spirituality Revolution* (HarperCollins) prior to coming to Australia, but I discovered his work *Re-Enchantment* (HarperCollins) whilst visiting and highly recommend it.

Tacey observes that many people have begun to separate the very concept of 'spirituality' from the structures of organised religion. Virtually nothing has remained immune from the disillusioning forces of modernity; nothing has escaped the appearance of being arbitrary, contrived and corrupted by egotism or human voice. He sees the new Australian spirituality as a protest movement against the established national ego, buttressed by its social and church infrastructure. He thinks that society has relied too long on the soul that was imported from Europe; and that experiments in the spiritual realm, not just receiving conventional church dogma, would suit the Australian temperament and enthusiasms.

Tacey suggests that Australia is experiencing 'colonisation in reverse'.

> The land we thought dull and inert, an empty field upon which we would stamp our own authority, is proving to have a spiritual authority far greater than our own. We are witnessing the rebirth of an ancient experience of the spirit. The spirit is holistic, embodied, mystical, and immanental rather than transcendental. And while the process has only just begun, and will take a great deal more time to be realised, Australia could provide important spiritual leadership to the Western world,

because what we are undergoing here is a
transformation that all Western nations will
eventually have to undergo if civilisation is to
recover a creative relationship with the earth . .
. The popular Celtic revival is a positive sign
that an earth-based, celebrative spirituality is
already growing in parts of the West. [3]

Re-imagining Christianity

During my Australian trip I met Tim Costello. In *Tips From a
Travelling Soul-Searcher* (Allen & Unwin) he quotes from Ivan
Illich:

Neither revolution nor reformation can
ultimately change society—rather you must tell
a new and powerful tale, one so persuasive that
it sweeps away the old myths and becomes the
preferred story—one so inclusive that it gathers
all the bits of our past and present into a
coherent whole, and shines light into the future
so we can take one step forward.[4] In the
beginning God imagined, and the cosmos came
to birth. We are designed to reflect God, and as
we imagine, the new comes to birth.

I found that my college and church lectures on 'Re-Imagining
Christianity' resonated with those present. We re-imagined
Christianity as a tree with many small branches, twigs and
leaves. It has three main branches: Orthodox, Roman Catholic
and Protestant. Much old growth is falling to the ground.
Radical pruning is going on. Below the three main branches is
one great trunk—the undivided universal church. Underneath
the soil is a hidden root system. The dying and pruned parts of

the tree have become disconnected from these roots. They have ceased to draw nutrients from the soil.

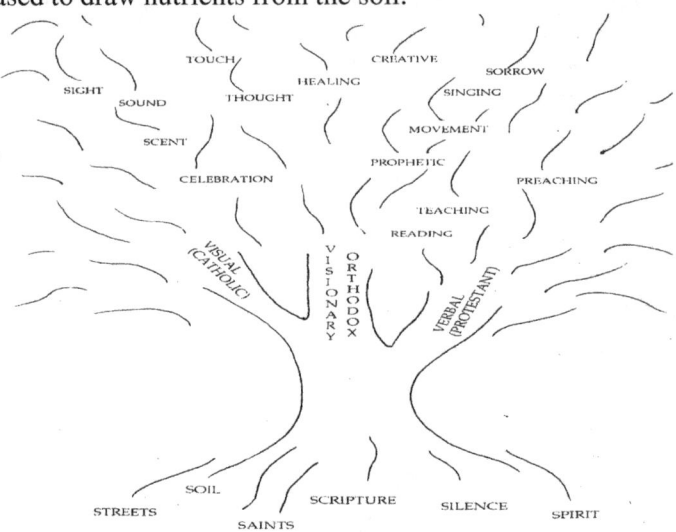

Some of these roots are what new seekers of spirituality look for, but assume are not to be found in churches. These roots include silence and contemplative prayer, creation spirituality, discernment of spirits, discovering God within, justice and beauty—as well as scriptures and sacrament, saints and seasons. As church people re-connect with these roots the tree becomes fruitful and endogenous growths take place. One day these will be seen as the norm.

I found myself addressing my audiences as 'Dear Australian oak trees'. This is because I discovered that the Australian oak tree does not grow upwards or outwards in its first years, it grows only downwards. Only when its roots reach the water table does it branch out—and then it survives many years of drought.

The emerging church will connect with the Australian temperament

In USA they say 'No problem', in UK they say 'No way', but in Australia they say 'No worries'. Behind this ubiquitous phrase lies a sunny disposition. People in Australia, unlike in many other countries, seem to actually enjoy life—the sun, the light, the outdoors. The mechanics of living, which people in many lands are in thrall to, loom less large than the living itself. There is much to be enjoyed and perhaps that is why Australians are typically happy and have a twinkle in the eyes!

Australians also talk straight. 'You lied to me' an airport baggage clerk told me after I failed to correct her assumption that my computer bag had a computer in it. In fact it was packed with stuff which would have been confiscated from the main bag as over-weight. A civilised society has officials who are honest and concerned to do the right thing. In most parts of Australia there is little fear of being cheated or robbed in travel centres, shops or parks. I was also surprised by 'men's talk' when driving 'with the lads' to Melbourne's Boxing Day Test Match. It began with 'Do you want to hear my testicle story?' Australians are happy to talk about bodily functions—unlike the British whose southerners, at least, are too repressed to talk about any such thing.

I found the republican spirit is alive and well in Australia, and it is quite widely assumed that the monarchy will soon be replaced. Mere replacement, however, would be a let-down. The republican replacement of British monarchy will only be life-giving if it becomes a means of expressing and sustaining inclusiveness and roots, justice and mystery, achievement and spirit. I hope my Australian friends will not under-estimate the value of such traits as these. They may not be everything, but many parts of the world need them.

The emerging church will embrace 'the shadow'

A highlight of my visit was a week with the Holy Transfiguration Community in Geelong, for whose generous hospitality, rich liturgy, and depth of honest friendship I shall always be grateful. This is a community where all social action and relationships rise out of daily dense silence and stillness, and whose contemplative worship is both contemporary and heavily influenced by Orthodox theology and music. The Community started as the Baptist church for the area, but became a seven-day-a-week monastic community which now includes Christians from other communions. Its hospitality is inclusive of all people and faith traditions. It is financially totally self supporting and so offers its hospitality free of charge.

I found this model of the Church unique in one respect: their dedication to daily work with their 'shadow'. This aspect of ourselves, as explored by CJ Jung, is the part that we bury because we find it unacceptable. It has both a positive and a dark destructive face. These brothers and sisters address the shadow and by so doing, have become more authentic presences in the world. The transfiguration of Jesus, to them, is an expository insight into the meaning of salvation and redemption for them. In Jungian wisdom, the idea of Transfiguration is important as well—whatever energy is not transformed (or transfigured) is transferred. These brothers and sisters are a sign that the renewal of the church does not lie in superficial experiments so much as in deep fidelity to the living essence of the church.

After dealing with their personal shadow for many years, this Community has now turned to face the dark corporate shadow behind their public persona. The challenge to face the corporate shadow is avoided only at our peril. When buried spiritual tendencies are not brought into the healing light, they manifest themselves in destructive ways. The world's very survival is threatened by 'sacred rage'. 'The more unconscious we are of the religious problem', wrote CJ Jung, 'the greater the danger of our putting the divine germ within us to some ridiculous or demonic use'.[5] The non-rational becomes dangerously activated only if we lack the cultural symbols to express and nurture it. To express religious life consciously is the best insurance policy against future distorted religious passion.

A church or a nation that is in denial about its past cannot become whole or fulfil its destiny. Those parts of our past that lie buried because they are unacceptable need to be acknow-ledged. Inasmuch as they are still in our gene pool and continue to fester in dysfunctional behaviour patterns, they need also to be brought to God.

Learning from Aboriginal spirituality

Something within me said that to embrace the corporate 'shadow' I must journey into the desert heartlands of Australia. 'Only alcoholics and mystics go there', someone informed me. So I went to the foot of Uluru, the sacred mountain of many Aboriginal people. I learned some of the Aboriginal dreams, but it seemed to me that the point is not to copy their dreams, but to learn from them how to dream. The Bible regards dreaming as part of the movement of God's Spirit among the people: 'Your young will see visions and your old will dream dreams' (Acts 2:17). This is about re-imagining the world with God.

I had discussions with various people about how certain insights of the Aboriginal people can be integrated with the existing church. In addition to the value of Dreamtime these insights include: awareness that we are all interconnected; the importance of silence; and the sacredness of the land.

I met Darren Cronshaw whose book *Credible Witness* (UNOH) brilliantly unpacks the history of mission in Australia and also picks up on the Aboriginal concept of *Dadirri*. Cronshaw says:

> This inner, deep listening and quiet still awareness is a traditional approach to contemplation that reflects deeply and listens to the land. *Dadirri* brings wholeness by enjoying the land, being attentive to the seasons, being together for ceremonies, listening to sacred stories and being at home in silence and in God's presence.[6]

Marlo Morgan's *Mutant Message Down Under: a Women's Journey into Dreamtime Australia* (HarperCollins) etches in my mind the power and possibility of intuition. She describes how after many weeks wandering with 'The Real People' through a mapless, trackless desert, without food or water supplies, they insisted it was her turn to lead the tribe for a day; only then could she be truly one of them. She was terrified. She had none of her western external aids; she had nothing but intuition. As day wore on, they grew weaker and death by thirst drew near. Still they insisted she must lead—and her intuition would guide her.

Finally, she let go of her left-brain conditioning. Into her right brain popped the apparently meaningless thought to put a rock she was carrying into her mouth. Miraculously, water came from it into her mouth. Then another illogical thought came to her: 'Be water'. She imagined, felt, talked water. As she walked she used all her senses. She could see, smell, and sense water. Across a large, flat plain only one small mound was in sight. She led the tribe to it. There was water, and survival. The leap of embracing her intuition and backing her hunches worked. The emerging church has to be the intuitive church.

Morgan suggests that 'The Real People' don't just give water or food to needy people, it is the feeling with which they do it which really counts. They believe that slowing down the body makes us aware of the really important wounds we need to mend: such as gaping holes in our belief system, walled up tumours of fear, eroding faith in our Creator and hardened emotions of unforgiveness.

I learned that Aboriginal ministers from the main churches have explored a Rainbow Spirit Theology (see *Rainbow Spirit Theology: Towards an Australian Aboriginal Theology* (HarperCollins: Sydney). They are glad that many Aboriginal people today affirm the positive message of the Gospel brought by missionaries, but they see the wholesale rejection of traditional culture as unnecessary and destructive. Because the Christian message was imposed from above and, like the strangler fig tree does in nature, choked the life out of the rich Aboriginal spiritual tradition, it also choked life out of the people themselves.

Are these things that we can and should integrate from Aboriginal spirituality?

> Not to possess but to live as guests of the sacred land.
> To be content with whatever we have
> To find pleasure in the simple pastimes of life
> To fear nothing of what can be taken from me
> To seek the wisdom of forebears and dreams.

Healing the wounded past

There are over six hundred Aboriginal tribes. Each has different myths and histories. There were conflicts between tribes and bad things within them. We should not romanticise. We cannot and should not copy their way of life. We can, however, acknowledge that the dreadful mistreatment of Aboriginal people in many, though not all parts of Australia has violated the dignity that belongs to every human group; and that the denial, the guilt and the dysfunctional behaviour patterns resulting from this mistreatment still fester.

The deepest wounds in Australia are still between the aboriginal peoples and the heirs of the settlers. The National Sorry Days, the creation of good reservations and of structures for the support of aboriginal art and development, and the inclusive approach of the churches and others have made a contribution towards healing. More is needed and I am aware that many creative avenues are being explored.

In relation to the Europeans, only the Aboriginals regard themselves as indigenous. But in relation to immigrants from Asia and the Middle East, only the Anglo-Celtic Australians regard themselves as indigenous. Everybody's forebears were once immigrants.

I was in Australia when violent confrontations broke out on Sydney's Cronulla beach between Anglo-Australian surfers and men of Lebanese Muslim origin who typically came there on the train. Worldwide newspaper headline focused on racist attitudes. However, a series of dialogues took place under different auspices. Kevin Manning, Catholic Bishop of Parramatta, and Keysar Trad, President of Australia's Islamic Friendship Association, began a series of dialogues, sometimes hosted by local committees. In Annangrove, Sydney's Bible belt, the local council overturned its decision to refuse planning permission for a Muslim prayer centre. Once open, this hosted a dialogue, which included the President of Australia's National

Council of Churches, on 'Forgiveness from a Muslim and Christian Perspective.'

Anzac church

The Anzac nations could be a bridge in a world threatened by a clash of civilisations. The spectre of the have nations (mainly Western and Christian) oppressing the have-not nations (mainly Eastern and Muslim) and destroying each other is horrifyingly real.

Another way is needed. This may be the rise of a form of Christianity that is based on service, not power, which re-connects us with the earth, the poor and the unseen world. Muslims will die for the idea of God ruling the world; we need Christians who will live for God to be discovered in every part of the world.

Each year Australia edges an inch nearer the eastern nations. The distance is minute, but could it be a divine parable: is it time for the Anzac nations to integrate the best of Western with the best of Eastern spirituality? Could its church become like a tree that is both truly indigenous and truly universal, and whose leaves are for the healing of both Western and Eastern nations?

Chapter 2

What is Dying?

Death: the final cessation of vital functions in an organism.
Oxford English Reference Dictionary

Death can come by a thousand cuts. The shelf life of second-millennium forms of church is nearing its end. Anachronistic practices and mind sets have accumulated which make these alien to a majority of the population.

Although the gates of hell shall never prevail against the essence of the universal church (Matthew 16:18), any particular form of that church can most certainly die. In his travel book *From the Holy Mountain* William Dalrymple observes many churches that have survived since the early centuries which are at this moment becoming relics.

The statistics of decline in Europe are wellknown and remorseless. According to the *World Christian Encyclopaedia* 53,000 'attenders' are leaving the church in Europe and North America every week.[7] Various more local surveys conducted since 1982 indicate that if anything the decline is increasing.[8] The 1990 European Values Study showed that some seventy-one per cent claimed to believe in God, sixty-eight per cent in the soul, fifty-four per cent defined themselves as religious people. Active members of churches are 14.4 per cent of the population—regular churchgoing is under half that figure.

Church of Scotland statistics published in the mid 1990s indicated that if the decline in membership continued, there would be no members left by the year 2024. The church is losing 18,000 members a year.

The same can be said for churches in Australia with the Australian Bureau of Statistics reporting sixty-eight per cent of Australians identify as Christian and approximately 7.5 per cent attend church weekly (2001). There has also been at least a seven per cent drop in church numbers within a five-year period according to National Church Life Survey (2001).

RIP: The powerful church

Many people think that the Christendom style church is proceeding to die. This is an exciting time rather than a time for mourning. We have a chance to lose the shackles that have bound us to positions of power rather then identifying with the humble Jesus of Nazareth.

RIP: What the retreating church needs to discard

The retreating church needs to discard attitudes and practices that have crept in which were not of God, and which have put up barriers between the church and the people. Prejudices, cloaked in the garb of doctrine, which may have helped people in previous cultures to understand the Faith, took the place of love and lack the suppleness that characterises living truth.

John Sumner dialogues at Glastonbury with similar groups of former churchgoers. From such encounters we can draw up a list such as this:

Twenty things that make good people angry with
the church

Lack of humanity
Lack of integrity
Lack of spiritual depth
Lack of a generous spirit
Lack of tolerance of people who differ from them
Lack of forgiveness
Lack of imagination
Lack of awareness
Misuse of power
Engendering of false guilt
Mistreatment of the earth
Belittling of sexuality
Neglect of key life moments
Non- inclusive leadership
Misrepresentation of the nature of salvation
Misrepresentation of the nature of sin
Misrepresentation of heaven, hell and the other world
Wordy, preachy church services
Pressurised mission approaches
Abuse of power

We are seen to lack integrity. No, not the accusations of the
sensational press, not the intolerance that expects clergy and
church to be perfect each twenty-four hours, not the guilt and
hate that delights to see priests fall. No, that hurts but I don't
mean any of that.

We stand accused of dishonesty in several ways:

Dishonesty in our reading of the Bible
Dishonesty in talking about God

Dishonesty in our assessment of others
Dishonesty in our assessment of wealth and power

Postmodern people distrust big claims that do not connect with one's own story. They reject judgmental words about others that do not connect with one's own vulnerability. They despise talk about love of neighbour by people and churches who do not connect with the poor.

RIP: God in the box

Organisms begin to die when they no longer respond to their environment. Richard Harries, Bishop of Oxford has written about God outside the box. Churches have become boxed in. The framework (the world view) in which they are set has changed out of recognition in the last thirty years. Some sociologists relate the emergence of 'new plausibility structures' to processes of religious change. PL Berger refers to the arrival on the world stage of new perspectives, elements and questions with regard to reality, existence and life itself, to which old religious explanations and structures no longer correspond.[9] The dying church relates to the old framework. The emerging church relates to the new.

> We are entering a new age. The European civilisation which we have known for the past two thousand years is giving way to a global civilisation.
>
> Bede Griffiths

A paradigm is the mental framework into which we fit everything we know. In most aspects of life—scientific, social, cultural, economic, ecological, psychological, and religious— we no longer understand our world as did our forbears even until recently the world and its institutions are going through the biggest shift for hundreds, perhaps thousands of years.

This has profound implications for churches. All the second millennium church streams have telltale signs of a mind-set which is becoming obsolete. This vast paradigm shift means that the form church has taken in the west for centuries now needs fundamental reappraisal.

RIP to the patriarchal church

> There is the possibility that religions, in the form that we know them, belong to the age of Patriarchy (c 8000BC to 2000 CE).
>
> Diarmuid O'Murchu[10]

> Our culture is engaged in a tremendous reappraisal of the intuitive, of the feminine, of everything affecting or concerning subjectivity . . . Every indication exists that we are witnessing the emergence of one of the key archetypes of humanity's collective unconscious: the anima, in all of its multiple manifestations. A like event occurs only once every several thousand years. And when it occurs, the axis of history suffers a universal shock, as men and women once more produce a new self-interpretation and redefine their interpersonal relations.
>
> Leonardo Boff[11]

The feminisation of society means that feelings have now won proper public respect alongside rationality. Sign, symbol, and intuition are now seen to be essential to explain the whole dimension of reality. These need to be embraced, though negative aspects of feminisation such as gender confusion, crisis in masculinity and denial of motherhood also need to be addressed.

An article by Francis Fukuyama in *The Financial Times* was headed 'The Death of Hierarchy'. He argues that the flow of information is changing authoritarian forms of organisation in the workplace. They are being replaced by flat or networked organisations where shared values are the key.[12] The patriarchal, top-down, or one-shape fits all type of church has had its day.

RIP to a monochrome church

Culturally accepted norms of a generation ago are now questioned. Some of these changes, especially as they affect a church context, have been expressed like this:

Monologue ⟶ Interaction

Cerebral ⟶ Visual

Consumerism ⟶ Simplicity

Explanation ⟶ Experience

Status   ⟶ Service

Activism ⟶ Mysticism

Linear Thinking   ⟶ Bit thinking

Believing ⟶ Belonging

Argument ⟶ Story

Reductionism ⟶ Holism

Standardisation ⟶ Personal choice

External authority ⟶ Inner conviction

RIP to a non-ecological church

> The Western world is into a deep cultural
> pathology as we enter the terminal phase of the
> Cenozoic period.
>
> Thomas Berry[13]

Thomas Berry, the Roman Catholic Passionist priest, creationist
and research director, calls for a massive shift from an
anthropocentric to a biocentric view, if the planet is to survive
as we know it. In recent decades a wide range of groups have
emerged—conservationists, single issue campaigners and those
into deep ecology—who realise this truth.

RIP to a fragmented church

The second-millennium forms of church are not only anachronistic, they are also fragmented. Few Christians under forty
want their identity to be tied to a protest movement that
occurred over four hundred years ago, that is, to be labelled
either Catholic or Protestant. We are living at the end of the era
in which the Catholic/Protestant divide at the Reformation was
the dominating framework of the Western church. Christians
are sensing that the Reformation represented not only a split in
doctrine and organisation, but also a split in the western
'Christian' psyche. Now that the false splits between
organisation and mysticism, between the whole and the parts,
are beginning to heal in the corporate psyche, the churches have
to catch up.

RIP to dehumanising tendencies

Second millennium churches neglected the biblical Wisdom
tradition in Christianity, which values the feminine in God and
in people. Towers, tasks and tirades became their landmarks.

From the churches the people gained a vague impression that God was like a mean boss who tries to find out what people are doing in order to tell them not to.

Church people have been conditioned for centuries to disguise their innermost being. This point is tellingly made in Ronald Ferguson's biography of the Scottish Presbyterian minister George McLeod, who, he says 'was keeping strict controls on access to his innermost core, where the puritan carefully policed the passionate. The language of one's innermost feelings was not in the McLeod family lexicon . . . he had the McLeod reputation of omni-competence to protect and uphold.'[14] After a break down George had a transforming experience, which enabled him thereafter to model a Christianity which helped people to become more fully human.

RIP to misuse of power

In his speech accepting the honour of a Union Medal from the Union Theological Seminary, New York, George McLeod said: 'The love of power has ruled the world, temporal and ecclesiastical, since the beginning of time. The Roman Empire was created by the love of power. The Roman Church got pre-eminence through the love of power. The love of power invaded John Knox in his desire to recover power for the new church' (at the Reformation in Scotland). 'Now science has given new meaning to power with nuclear weapons. Thus power has jettisoned morality. So this is indeed the Church's hour. Only one force is sufficient for our day. It is the power of love.'

CJ Jung correctly diagnosed the future Nazi threat in Germany, because he understood that in that country's collective unconscious Christianity was a religion that had been imposed, and was therefore only on the surface. As a result paganism, which had been repressed rather than redeemed, was poised to make a come back in destructive new form.[15]

If we are to avoid the tragedy of an imposed, unnatural form of Christianity being replaced by a natural but unredeemed paganism we need to understand the context of our times.

Gardens of Love

I went to the Garden of Love,
And saw what I never had seen:
A Chapel was built in the midst,
Where I used to play on the green.

And the gates of this Chapel were shut,
And 'Thou shalt not' writ over the door;
So I turned to the garden of love
That so many sweet flowers bore,

And I saw it was filled with graves,
And tomb-stones where flowers should be;
And Priests in a black gowns were walking their
    rounds,
And binding with briars my joys and desires.

William Blake

RIP to defensive church leaders

Why are so many churches defensive rather than loving?

John Sumner writes of his experience of the training of leaders in his church:

Unable to love myself, my capacity to love others is reduced. I have protective barriers between me and real human people. Videos, schemes, dress, housing, categorised ways of thinking, plans of Salvation, committee-made prayers.

And because of my low self-confidence, I cannot see how to utilise the thoughts, the questions, the explorations, and the expertise of others who do not fit my trained schemes and thought-forms. We may have head teachers, speech tutors, senior managers, electronic technicians in our church, but I am so busy, so caught up in meeting ingrained expectations, that I cannot learn how to use them. We may have original thinkers, deep questioners, far-seeing spirits in our circle, but unless I can fit them in to my system of concepts they had better be left unattended.

This negative experience was not universal amongst Theological Colleges. But I do believe it was widespread.

RIP to belittling of other religions

I love all religions. I am in love with my own.
Mother Teresa of Calcutta

E Stanley Jones, the missionary to India, once asked Mahatma Gandhi: 'How can we make the Christian faith more native to India, so that it is no longer something "foreign" which is associated with foreign governments and seen as foreign religious practice, but it becomes part of life in India and a faith that makes a powerful contribution to building up this country?'

Gandhi replied: 'Firstly, I would suggest that all Christians—missionaries and others—must start living more like Christ. Secondly, practise your faith without blurring it or watering it down. Thirdly, put special emphasis on love because it is the central point of Christian faith and therefore the decisive motivating force. Fourthly, study non-Christian religions with great sympathy, so that you can appeal to people of other faiths more effectively.'

RIP to denial

It is possible that what has already happened to traditional religious communities is now happening to churches. If so, we do well to heed what Gerald Arbuckle wrote in 1988:

> Many religious congregations today are in chaos. They are not sure about the meaning, contemporary relevance or mission of religious life and, on the practical level, they find it difficult to cope with often rapidly declining numbers, few or no vocations, and the rising average age of membership.
>
> Some congregations acknowledge that they are in chaos and are seriously concerned about wanting to do something about it. Others struggle to deny it, thinking it is just like a bad dream and very soon it will all disappear and 'things will be normal once more'. Other congregations, perhaps because they are still receiving vocations, for example Third World countries, think they are not in chaos. They may in fact be in deep chaos, because they complacently refuse to search for the inner meaning of religious life and how it must

respond with apostolic vitality to the pastoral needs of people today. They cannot at some point in the future escape the consequences of their prolonged denial.[16]

We have to face up to the sea change that is taking place. This is affecting even the largest charismatic churches. The leader of one such church says 'I can see it is dying underneath'.

The nature of dying before something can grow is a very biblical principle, 'a seed must die before it can grow'.

Chapter 3

What is Being Born Again?

A new generation of leaders

I shall never forget listening to some prophetic church leaders at a packed London meeting. The gist of what I remember is this: 'The First World War destroyed a whole generation of leaders. In the period since then the church has had a dearth of both able and God-inspired leaders. Seventy years has now passed. The ancient people of Israel had to spend seventy years in exile in Babylon, but after this period they returned and began to fulfil God's plans again. Britain's churches have been in a kind of Babylon. That period is ending. There are now many humble leaders who desire God's will; God is equipping them to do great things . . . '

Young Christians in Western lands are coming out of the woodwork in order to get training, some in established church centres, and others in new frameworks.

Change is being prophesied

We are now entering one of the greatest watershed periods in human history.

> Creation itself is charged with the electricity of
> these times and is beginning to groan and travail
> for what is about to come . . .

In preparation for this greatest of events the church is about to go through a metamorphosis.

She is going to change from a worm into a butterfly.

A caterpillar is confined to the earth, and its path must conform to the contour of the earth.

Likewise. for nearly two thousand years the church has often conformed more to the ways of the world than to the ways of the Spirit.

Soon the church will go through a change so dramatic that she will seem to emerge as an entirely different creature. It will be like another birth . . .

Rick Joyner[17]

A wave of fresh thinking

There has been a glut of books about the demise and the re-formation of the church. *Being Human: Being Church* by Robert Warren has challenged churches to turn into missionary congregations and into laboratories for becoming more fully human beings.[18] *Brave New Church* by that brave vicar of St Andrew's, Chorley Wood, diagnoses our society as a slave to various addictions. The church, too, has been addicted, he argues, but it is beginning to break free and become the agency, par excellence, which sets the people free from their addictions.[19]

In *New Tasks for a Renewed Church*[20] Tom Wright urges Christians to find the focal points of the emerging new paganism, and to find ways of honouring Jesus as Lord within these contexts. He calls for Christian 'shrines' to be established in various areas: By coming alongside those in pain as a result of war; by proclaiming in liturgy and deeds that the powers of Mammon shall be brought low and the needy shall be lifted up;

by celebrating sexuality as the glory of a relationship of integrity; by cherishing the earth; by developing forgiving and respectful friendships with people of other faiths within which witness becomes authentic; by restoring the Eucharist and a sacramental approach to the centre of church life; by rescuing from Eastern monopoly the mystical and contemplative traditions of prayer; and by restoring holism to intellectual endeavour.

In *Threshold of the Future: Reforming the Church in the Post-Christian West*, Mike Riddell gives examples of churches in his native New Zealand which are pioneering new ways of being church, from *Parallel Universe* to *Spine*.[21]

Repentance for the church's past sins

As the second millennium drew to a close some churches tried to identify significant wrong actions in the second millennium that lived on in distorted patterns, to say sorry and to put right what could be put right. They followed the example of Ezra and Nehemiah in the Old Testament.

If Christianity is to be a force for healing the world in the third millennium, the image of the Cross as a Sword, by which people of other faiths are forced to convert against their will must be expunged, and it must become again, as it was at the beginning, an image of unconditional love. Pope John Paul 11 called on his church to make penance for their mistreatment of Jews.

For millions of Muslims and Jews, the Cross symbolises the sword. So it is a wonderful thing that Christians from various backgrounds have made Reconciliation Walks along the route Crusaders took through Muslim lands to pray, to say sorry, to make friends. Mothers and children ran over to these walkers with tears and embraced them. A whole new set of dynamics was coming into play. If Christianity is experienced as a movement of unconditional love, who knows how far the healing of fragmentation may go in the Muslim and Christian worlds?

Churches in Australia took part in a 'National Sorry Day', in which schools and organisations throughout the land said sorry to the aboriginal people for the raping of their land and culture by the European invaders.

South Africa's Truth and Reconciliation Commission, headed by Archbishop Desmond Tutu was an historic example of this corporate healing process. The Anglican Church in Japan, at its synod in 1996, formally confessed its sin in having supported their country's colonial war of oppression in World War II. It says its first synod after the war 'should have deeply repented for not having fulfilled their prophetic role. They should also have made a sincere apology to their neighbours whom Japan had invaded and ruled, and should have sought a truly reconciled relationship with them . . . '

As pilgrims from Roman, Anglican, Reformed and New Church traditions gathered at Lindisfarne in 1997 during their journey from Rome to Iona, a confession in the following vein was made:

> We confess with shame
>> the loss in the church of integrity, humility
>>> and patience
>> the crushing of spontaneity
>> the caging of the wild Spirit
>> the breaking off of relationships
>> the bruising of the crushed reeds
>> the arrogance of the intellect
>> the pride of empire-building.

We accept our share of responsibility for these sins
    and seek to shed them on behalf of ourselves
    and our churches.
Lord, have mercy upon us and forgive us.

Re-birthing ancient truths

We are coming to the end of the parish phase of
church. It has happened before.

Bishop Ian Harland

Saint Patrick introduced the top-down diocesan system into
fifth century Ireland, for that was all he knew from his training
in the urban centres in Europe. Yet within a hundred years the
focus had changed from the bishop to the monastery, which was
led by a man or a woman. Bishops continued their sacramental
duties, but they were under the authority of the Abbott, who
looked after the organisation. The pattern of church
organisation followed the natural pattern of the people groups.

One ruling family after another embraced the Faith and gave
prime parts of their estates to be used as a monastery, which
became the hub of the tribal life. These early monasteries had
no barriers, apart from a ditch for practical reasons. There was
constant movement in and out by children, women and
labourers. There were no imposing buildings.

These monastery 'churches' were multi functional resource
centres. They served as prayer base, drop-in centre, library,
school, health center and psychiatric care centre. They were
totally open to outsiders. To them visitors brought the news of
the world. They related to the neighbourhood as guardians of
local culture, affirming it whether it was vibrant or dying,
though confronting certain bad practices such as wizardry. Even
within the monasteries there were all sorts of options. There
were clergy, lay monks and nuns with life vows, others with

temporary vows, and some who lived at home. Some were married.

The major Celtic monasteries were not built, as were the eastern ones, as an escape from the world. They were built on the main highways of sea and river and near large settlements; they were organised in order to penetrate the pagan world and to extend the church. The monasteries provided a God-given framework of prayer, work and rest, reflecting the rhythms of the natural and the Christian year. They were the main centres of hospitality and all Celtic Christians were taught to 'open their heart to Christ in the stranger'. They also introduced written education to Ireland and became centres of learning.

The early monastic churches marvellously modelled hospitality. St Benedict's Rule (number fifty-three) states that 'all guests are to be welcomed as Christ'. The eighth-century Rule of St Ailbe suggested that hospitality should consist of 'a clean house, a big fire, a good wash and a comfortable bed'. Some Celtic churches, such as Columba's monastery at Durrow, fed a thousand visitors a day.

At Bangor over 3,000 monks devoted themselves to the singing of Perennial Praise. Their praise book, the Bangor Antiphonary, which is preserved in the Ambrosian library, Milan, says 'Let the many keep awake in community on a third of the nights in the year in order to read aloud from the Book and to expound judgment and to sing blessings all together'.

Columba went into exile from the security of his beloved homeland and founded the Iona monastery on Scotland's western shore. True, this was a strategic place, but it was also on the edge. From the extremity of Iona Aidan brought a Mission to English barbarians, and established his church base on borderland between isle and mainland at Lindisfarne.

The many daughter churches he planted throughout the large kingdom of Northumbria, though inland, kept alive that same borderland spirit. Thus Cuthbert and Eata transferred from one Lindisfarne daughter church at Melrose to another at Ripon, were edged out when the Romanising prelate Wilfred took control, and having no worldly handles, returned to Melrose. Bede wrote of those Lindisfarne servants of Christ: 'None of them would accept lands or possessions to build monasteries, unless compelled to by the secular authorities.'

Why did people throng to the early Celtic communities, in Britain as much as in Ireland? The whole life of the monk, his service to guests, his work, his prayer, silence, rest, relations with his brothers were offered as a liturgy to the Holy Trinity. The physical pattern of the monastery bore witness to this reality. From the church and its holy altar all things proceeded, and to them all things returned. The huts, the refectory, the guest room, everything revolved around the hub which was the place of worship. Worship repeated each day and night, yet, for those who entered into it from the heart, it was not static. It was a single motion towards God; it had an inner dynamic which reflected God's rhythms and by which the soul moved upwards towards God, and raised all creation.

Monasteries in Britain were not other-worldly. They were a source of soul friendship and those outside the monasteries flocked to Aidan, Cuthbert, and Hilda. So also they did to David of Wales. Animals and children would wander around. In Anglo-Saxon England, monasteries became the nearest thing to a town. It was only later that this fell away. Pride of power and possessions, that ugly sore that hid under the veneer of religion, strutted across the church. The continual repentance of the heart, the daily immersion in Christ's Eucharistic self-giving, the sharing of goods in common became a distant memory.

Hermitage churches

Hermits went to the edges of rocks or lakes, and churches sprang up around them. Kevin, the tall, skin-wearing hermit of

Glendalough, chose to live in a sunless cave fifty feet above a lake inhabited by a wild creature; it was as if he needed to reach to the extremity of life in order to find the all-sufficiency of God. Around Kevin's cave grew up the seven churches of a monastic city.

A Breton *Life of St Gildas* tells how his sister and two of his brothers established a *skete* in a remote place. Each had their own dwelling and their own place of prayer, some distance apart. Each brother took it in turns to spend much of the day with his sister, sharing in the regular hours of prayer, Holy Communion, a meal, and no doubt in work or vigils. Each of the three returned to their own place before sunset and kept vigil in their own place of prayer. Evidently all sorts of people were drawn to them, for the author of *The Life* says they became famous for their constant miracles. No constant miracles without people![22]

The Hermitage, or *Skete*, was an alternative model to the central monastic church, and became widespread in Britain and in Ireland. The original intention was not to establish a hub church in an accessible place, but to find a quiet place away from busy places in which to serve God in an undisturbed rhythm of prayer and work. The by-product was that by a mysterious chemistry people who were tuned in to this life of deep peace were drawn to these places. They made there own dwellings in the same area, adopted a similar lifestyle, and shared in Holy Communion and meals on certain festival days. As years passed these became pilgrim centres and a form of church which met the need of many of the quiet types.

The Celtic church was culture friendly

None of the Celtic Christians who won over the indigenous population were martyred. This was not because they feared or favoured, but because they harnessed all that was Gospel-friendly in their culture to Christ.

'In Christ are hidden all the treasures of wisdom and knowledge' (Colossians 2:3). Celtic Christians incorporated wisdom from the Druids who had the wisdom of nature. The Celtic missionaries said God had given people two books, the book of Scripture and the book of creation. The Druids had a deep intuition. There is an Irish story that on the day of Christ's crucifixion King Conchubar noticed the eclipse of the sun and asked the Druid Bucrach the cause of this sign. 'Jesus Christ, the Son of God, who is now being crucified by the Jews', replied the Druid. Christians recognised that the intuition of their best forbears was in tune with Christ even before they had been taught about him. The sixth-century century Welsh bard Taliesin declared: 'Christ, the Word from the beginning, was from the beginning our teacher . . . there never was a time when the Druids of Britain held not its doctrines.' As a baptised boy Columba was taught by a Druid; as an adult he supported measures to strengthen the institution of the bards, yet he tried to lead both Druids and their pupils to Christ. 'Christ is my druid', he told them. Later it was the Irish monks who first wrote down the pre-Christian folk stories which continued traditional wisdom.

The Irish were led to transfer their veneration from the High King of Ireland to the High King of Heaven; from the sun to the Sun of suns. On standing stones in Ireland Christians placed an arrow to lead the passer by from the sun disc which pagans had engraved on one side, to the disc of Christ transcending the sun which Christians had engraved on the other side. Christ is placed in the centre of the sun circle on most old Christian Celtic crosses.

Celtic believers Christianised the pagan seasons. The pagan blessing of the lustral waters on the sixth of January became

the Epiphany which commemorated Jesus' immersion in the
waters. Candles were held to the throat for healing on the first
day of the Celtic Spring, and this became St Brigid's Day.
Christians continued the Druids use of ashes as a sign of
purification. The veil between earth and heaven was at its thin-
nest on Samhain, the first day of winter's dark: Christians filled
it with the splendour of All Saints Day. The early church
assimilated the Greek wisdom. Celtic Christians incorporated
wisdom from the Druids. Our church has to assimilate the
wisdom of the best neo pagans of today.

   We, who for the first time since those days live in a pre-
dominantly pagan population, do well to learn from the Celtic
Christians, who in effect said to their pagan contemporaries:
'Come with your festivals that celebrate the elements, and we
will transform them into festivals for the Lord of the elements.
Come with your long flowing hairstyles—when we become
Christian monks we will keep these hairstyles because they give
glory to God. Come with your clans and natural networks of
association, and we will plant Christian communities of prayer
that go with the grain of these networks. Come with your
excitement about the after world, but let us see how the risen
Son of God throws light upon it. Come with your hunger for
worship and the world of the Spirit, and we will explain how
idols have no place now, because the God of gods has revealed
himself to us . . .'

Their leaders

The leaders of monastic churches were the natural leaders of the
people. They were usually members of extended ruling families
who made a life commitment to Christ. There were exceptions.
Ciaran was the son of a carpenter, but his physical and spiritual
stature was so exceptional that Columba thought the whole of

Ireland would follow him. He founded the monastic church at Clonmacnoise which flourished for a thousand years.

Women leaders were given equality of regard in the church. The leaders of the early large monasteries for both women and men were invariably women. The manner in which male church leaders addressed their female counterparts in the Celtic period is that of brother to sister.

The Saxon minster model

The Anglo Saxons continued the monastic churches, and many of them had the feel of a family. An information board at Brecon Cathedral, Wales, describes how, before the Normans took over, the cathedral was a mother community to a network of smaller churches. These were known as a *clas*, meaning that they were part of one family.

The Saxon monasteries, however, were increasingly regulated by bishops with a territorial responsibility—and people with inspirations for fresh monastic churches could not follow the patterns of the people so easily as before. The scholar monk Bede recommended that Bishop Ecbert should put down monasteries that did not toe the line with his diocese. This was a contrast to the bishops in the Celtic Mission who place themselves under the authority of an abbot and who did not have the power to veto monastic developments.

A focus for the multiplying churches in Saxon Britain was the Minster. This was a large church building that was both a multi resource centre and a community of clergy and other helpers who serviced the outlying churches. It was, of course, tied in to the national church's chain of command, and it perhaps became too 'clericalised' over time; but it is a model which is being looked to again.[23]

It was the Normans who finally obliterated the sense of the inclusive, grass roots family in the church. The tone of church leaders after the Norman Conquest was quite different. Much of the post Norman *Ancrene Wisse* (*Guide for Anchoresses*), for example, is written so that women shall know their place in a masculine hierarchy and society.[24]

The modern rediscovery of Celtic style churches

In his book *The Celtic Way of Evangelism: How Christianity can reach the West, Again*, George Hunter III, of Asbury Theological Seminary USA, argues that the Reformed churches, as well as the Roman Catholic churches of the USA, have continued the 'Roman paradigm' with dire results. He thinks that most leaders of America's churches are in denial, and continue to assume that control from headquarters, and the culturally European paradigm, are best for churches every-where. He believes that if western church leaders 'are willing to learn from a once-great Movement outside of the Roman paradigm, then Christianity can become contagious once more across North America and Europe in the twenty-first century'.[25]

Ordinary people are often more apt to pick this up than are their church leaders:

> We never knew this existed, but it's what we've always thought. We've always felt there is something more. We've been so oppressed by the Roman ways of the church. It's the natural way to live for people in this land.
>
> Joe O Siorain

This desire to recover a Celtic style of church is spreading across the world. I receive many letters and emails that indicate this. 'Having found this Celtic way of life I realise that is what I've always believed, but this has put it into words for me. I never knew it existed. Why didn't the church tell me?' wrote one person, 'Can you tell me of any church that follows this way?'

In the US Tom Sine, the author and Christian Futures Consultant, aims to develop a Celtic style community led by three couples, where students can gain an experience of living in a rhythm of prayer, work, study and relationship. A church leader from Austin, Texas identifies a similar need. In order to 'detoxify' people from 'the disease for degrees' which treats people as if they are not valid unless they accumulate paper certificates, she seeks Celtic style centres where people learn in a holistic, unpressured way through experience, prayer, relationship, intuition, as well as from books.

Clergy come to Lindisfarne in search of this new way. They arrive as apparatchiks, rushing from pillar to post. They yearn to become people who are tuned in. Some establish a daily pattern of stillness and prayer. Others already have this, but it has become an insulation from the rest of the day, rather than a way of being fully present to God and to others, throughout the day.

The well known conference speaker David Pawson issued a cassette entitled 'de-Greecing the church', in which he complains about the pagan influence of neo Platonism on the early church via Augustine of Hippo. After listening to this, a Cambridge scientist wrote: 'His complaints exactly echo your own complaints about what happened to the Celtic church following Augustine of Canterbury. The dynamism of Celtic Christianity is therefore precisely that of what is called "the early Church" (that is in Mediterranean lands).'

Lessons we can draw from these early models

We cannot, of course, recreate the organisation of the early Celtic church, nor should we. But it is possible to learn from them. It was Archbishop Michael Ramsay, quoting Arnold Toynbee, that great historian of the rise and fall of civilisations, who distinguished between historical movements based on archaism, and those based on transfiguration. As we grasp something of the mind-set and dynamic of the Church in Celtic lands, we can move forward in a way that transforms.

The nature of Celtic style churches today

How much of what is meant by 'Celtic style church' today actually correlates with what existed in the church of the fifth to the tenth centuries is a matter of debate. Documents are fragmentary, much is not certain, and in any case opportunities then were more limited. This does not invalidate the use of the term 'Celtic' as a symbol for today. For symbols accrue energies, and some key features of the early church in Celtic lands have become symbols which now bear their own life.

What do people mean by a Celtic style church? I often say that Celtic style churches have 'the three R's':

> Rhythm with God
> Roots in the land; and
> Rapport/Relationship with the people.

There is growing consensus that Celtic style churches weave together biblical, charismatic, and catholic strands.

Are they for cities? Yes, for Celtic style churches make connections between their surroundings and God, and are fully attentive to whoever and wherever they are. Wherever there can be a rainbow overhead, there a Celtic style church can be.

The following collection of attributes is drawn from all sorts of workshops and conversations. They may be thought of as the aspirations of many people who are drawn to the current 'Celtic' wave.

CELTIC STYLE CONGREGATIONS ARE:

In God
Holistic
Communal
Grassroots
Hospitable
Endogenous
Non-sectarian
Culture friendly
Creation friendly
Creative and poetic
Deep but not overlaid
At home with the body
Concerned for the poor
Single minded in mission
Disciplined yet spontaneous
Rhythmic in prayer and work
Adaptable to their environment
Genuine towards other churches
Heartfelt and natural in worship
Simple and uncluttered in life-style
Familiar with the world of the Spirit
In continuity with the original church
Incarnational without being parochial
At peace with neighbours and animals

THEY ARE FREE FROM:
clutter and artificiality
legalism and clericalism
wordy, stereotyped worship
hidden or defensive agendas
triumphalist or competitive attitudes

Roots for renewal

A person who is secure in their roots is free to explore the future. So is a church.

The Old Testament church had roots in the land and in the saving acts of God in its people. First millennium churches had roots in their Jewish parentage and in the apostles of their own lands.

An endogen is a plant in which new wood is developed in the interior of the stem: an endogenous church grows within the life of the people of its land. The last time the churches of Britain and Ireland were truly endogenous was the period of the Celtic Mission. Second Millennium churches became disconnected from the grass roots patterns of the people, from the communal memory and from the earth itself. Third Millennium churches will reconnect with these.

Carl Jung helps us understand the collective unconscious of peoples. For example, he understood Germany as a country of two levels. The surface level was Christian, but since Christianity had originally been forced upon it at the point of a sword, this was thin. The lower level was the pagan gods, which, taking vengeance after Germany was humiliated at the Treaty of Versailles would now break the bonds of its underground prison and take over, wreaking terrible havoc. Hitler plugged into the collective unconscious of seventy-eight million Germans. The emerging church has to plug into the collective unconscious, not to repress its basic instincts, but to transform them

Chapter 4

Needed Features for Emerging Churches

Listening and journeying

The church of the Old Testament was a people on the move, who .listened to God for direction. Although the desert travel phase ended, they habitually sang songs of ascent on the way up to the temple. Their temptation, like ours, was to get stuck, but prophets constantly urged them to walk humbly with their God. The members of the New Testament church were first called followers of The Way (Acts 9:2). Indeed, church tradition recognises the importance of journey. In some places the Rite of Initiation into the Roman Catholic Church is popularly known as 'The Journey'.

In the new way of being church, programmes and buildings are provisional; they flow out of Spirit-led initiatives, and when that tide ebbs they are beached. Thus there is space to hear God for the new thing God wants to do. Churches that live this way are not afraid to cross new frontiers. Sometimes this means asking God to show them an opportunity they are meant to take or a need they are meant to respond to.

The British composer John Tavener, who was converted to the Orthodox faith in 1976, says that the churches of the West will be unable to recover their mission until they recover humility, which he feels the churches of the East have not lost in the same way. One way the Western churches can recover this humility is to recover the idea of pilgrimage as a way of mission as well as of life. Celtic Christians went into exile from the safety and power zones of their homes in order to walk with nothing but Jesus in their hearts. Because they were so vulnerable, so mobile and so full of Jesus many of the pagans they befriended became Christians. John Finney, in his book *Recovering the Past: Celtic and Roman Mission*[26] concludes that more people became Christian this way than through organised missions.

One church leader tells me that his congregation has two types of people: 'position' people, who know what their position is and are against receiving from any one who does not hold it; and 'boom and bust' people, who have an experience of the Spirit, then take time out when it goes wrong. He wants to bring a third sort into being: the person on a journey who receives from God and mentors others.

I have been told of churches in USA who take youngsters away climbing and walking. They are each given a staff, newly cut. As they walk they talk freely about their childhood. They are free to ask questions about their sexuality, money, anything. They are encouraged to talk about what they have found difficult as infants, juniors, at home, with parents, peers, and schools. Each time they become aware of important points of their journey they mark it on their staff. In the evenings they will talk about these. And pray. Before they leave they will throw their staff on to a fire to be burned. In this way they marked that they are leaving their childhood. They make a commitment to Christ.

A church in Birmingham set up a Voice of the People Trust. The Rev Dr Laurie Green, Principal of the Aston Clergy Training Course, wrote of this:

> The 'Voice of the People' . . . comes from a
> deeply felt Christian concern that since all of us
> are made in God's image, then we should all be
> listened to . . . 'The Voice' tries to act as a
> vehicle for working class values and working
> class culture to be expressed . . . The powers that
> be will learn a lot from listening to the Cry of the
> City just as in the Bible, time and again, it was
> the cry of the people at the bottom of the pile that
> was the voice that God listened to and upon
> which God acted.

Many residents perceive the local church as a privatised
concern for a minority. They do not feel the church is in
solidarity with their good, even though non-religious,
aspirations. Businesses and political parties conducted listening
exercises in order to respond more effectively to the people
they were trying to reach, so is there any good reason why we
churches should not listen?

When a church truly listens to the cries of the people and to
the cries of its God it becomes, in the words of Dr Philip Potter,
a former President of the World Council of Churches, the
prophetic conscience of society.

A daily rhythm of prayer, work and re-creation

> To my mind, tradition is a God-given awareness of
> natural rhythms and of a fundamental harmony.
>
> Prince Charles

Tragically, the worship of most churches consists of packaged
words that do not so much as say hello to the sun's dawning,
the rain's falling, or the day's dying. Or else the worship spills

out of the surfeited psyches of dominant members who are too surfeited to notice the rhythms of their own bodies, let alone of the days or the years. Yet it is possible to create a sense of daily rhythm which touches and inspires a wider number, even amongst the most mobile populations, and which connects them with the ebb and flow of deeper realities.

The Bible sets the entire story of God's saving work for humanity within a universe of rhythm. The Bible tells how God chooses a people and teaches them ways of reflecting that rhythm in their society: through one day and one year in seven rest: the daily of prayer that reflects, the sun's rising and setting. The New Testament presents Jesus the model for human beings, living a rhythm of total self-giving to the people and total withdrawal to a solitary place. The Saviour arranged for his most significant actions to coincide with the rhythm of the religious seasons.

In emerging churches corporate worship follows the rhythm of the natural seasons and of the church year, and observes seasons of fasting or spiritual warfare, of lamentation for the sins and hurts of society, and of joy and celebration of creation. The word rhythm comes from a Greek word (*suthmos*) whose root meaning is flow.

Physicists are discovering that our universe has an under-laying pattern; nature is full of symmetry. Rhythm is indivisible. There is a rhythm of the seasons of the year, and a rhythm of the seasons of life. There is a rhythm between mas-culine and feminine. The emerging churches seek to flow in these rhythms.

A well known church leader told a 'New Wine' gathering that his church would have a holiday period in July and August because that is the natural thing to do. Then it would have more energy to develop programmes in the new autumn season.

Many things in life can be harnessed to rhythm. West Indian bands harness modern technology to serve their rhythmic music. Cassian's Institutes, section two, reveals that in monastic worship a cantor would sing ten verses of a psalm while everyone else listened. This was followed by silent prayer and a collect. There were four cantors who took turns to sing the psalms.

The first council of the New Testament churches saw these churches as a restoration of King David's set-up, and a making good the gaps in it (Acts 15:16). This, without doubt, included the restoration of daily worship.

> If this daily offering of total worship does not again become the centre of our life, our world will not be able to be transfigured or united. It will be incapable of surpassing its divisions, its imbalance, its emptiness and death, in spite of all human-centred plans to improve it.
> Archimandrite George Capsanis of Mount Athos.

In the first millennium the daily prayer together in the larger, hub churches was normal, and these were called 'Peoples Services'. However, they degenerated. Monastic churches developed long, wordy services which suited celibate monks but which put off the general population.. Daily worship in central churches became clericalised, form became more important than fellowship, ritual more important than relationship. A counter church culture developed which encouraged prayers from pulpits or in groups, but not corporate daily prayer.

In the third millennium, we have to make good the gaps, integrating the creativity and spontaneity of occasional prayer gatherings, with the first millennium's rhythm of corporate daily prayer. This is beginning to happen, in churches of all shapes and sizes. Some use Anglican or Roman Catholic liturgies. Others use simpler, more flexible patterns. Daily prayer patterns from contemporary communities such as Aidan and Hilda, Iona, Northumbria and Taize are increasingly being adopted.

St Patrick's Church, in downtown Hove, Sussex had a large Victorian building which was nearly redundant. The Bishop of Chichester invited four monks from the Community of the Servants of the Will of God to buy a nearby three storey terraced. They transferred three of their daily services of worship into the church. The monks gave homeless and hungry people hospitality, according to their Rule, but since they had too little space to meet the need, the rear of the church building was converted into a Shelter for the homeless and meals were provided following the midday and evening services. Pews were removed and icons put in their place. Soon not only the poor attended daily prayer, but suited business people came out of the woodwork too.

In the light of the link between their monastic house and St Patrick's the Abbot of the Community, Father Gregory, wrote Living for the Kingdom; a Rule for the Parish Community which integrates all aspects of church life into the Lord's Supper. There is a weekly rhythm of daily prayer together, a common meal on Thursday, fasting and prayer round the Cross on Friday, and regular blessings in homes.

Hospitality

The fundamental need of our society is to have men and women who together create communities of welcome.

Jean Vanier

Lack of hospitality has been the constant charge of God against his people. Many churches welcome newcomers at the door on Sunday, but these are not welcomed into the other rooms, as it were, during the week. Twentieth century churches tended to welcome people as believers: emerging churches welcome them as neighbours. In a people's church there is a welcome throughout the week, a place to be alone, to pray, to share a meal, to be listened to. There are displays and facilities which children, old people, business people, deaf people can relate to.

I have often asked church leaders if they know anywhere which does this today. They have told me of Sikh temples which do this, but not of a Christian church. Nevertheless, a growing number of churches do sponsor lunch clubs, refreshments or cafes. Many of these are not, however, part of a whole experience. In a monastic style church, lunch guests do not have to leave when the lunch club closes, they can stay to pray, wander, study or talk to people who are always there, in the atmosphere of a spiritual home.

The early British churches hosted the main social events in their area. All who lived and worked in the vicinity of the monastic church would be welcomed to the large barn with a blazing fire when an instrument, would be passed round. Each could take a turn to sing or play. The modern equivalent to this is the karaoke. Generally, pubs host these rather than churches. Emerging churches will host karaoke and barbecues.

I shall never forget touring Poland in the 1980s. Despite the fact that it was then behind the Iron Curtain, large numbers of young Catholics from other countries traversed the land with rucksacks on their backs, and slept on the floors of church halls, where they also used the kitchen and wash facilities. This contrasts with Britain where the youth hostel movement is divorced from the church. Peoples' churches have hostels.

Hospitality is not only about accommodation, it is also about creating emotional space. People now go to retreat houses who have ceased to go to churches. The reason, according to Paddy Lane of the National Retreat Association, is that retreat houses provide them with a welcoming, safe context where that which is of God in them can be drawn out; whereas churches put upon them sermons, hymnbooks, noise and churchy agendas. Monastic style churches provide both physical and emotional space.

Hospitality is a sign that a community is alive, that it is not afraid, that it has something valuable to share. To welcome anyone is always a risk; an over busy community which opens its doors can become a burned out community. There is a time for a community, as for an individual, to be alone, to deepen its identity and its intimacy with God; but there is also a time to open wide the doors.

Hospitality is a way of way of life that is due for a comeback. It is the smile that greets friend and stranger. It is the warm embrace, and the welcome of each person as a gift from God.

Human and healing

> God made us human beings not human doings.
>
> Robert Warren

In the film *Dances with Wolves* the Native American Chief Kicking Bear says to a US Army Chief: 'Of all the trails in life there is one that matters more than all the others. It is the trail of the true human being.' How many of our churches are on that trail?

What does it mean to be fully human? Here are some answers I have received to this question:

to be real
to make good relationships
to be a good lover
to be sensual, understanding, and beautiful inside
to be in touch with your feelings
to flow in your potential
to have masculine-feminine balance
to be healthy in mind and body
to be free
to live and die well
to appreciate good food, friends, and things
to appreciate the wonder of life
being alive with all your senses
to be deep but full of fun.

An Indian elder (Oriah Medicine Dreamer) put it this way:

I want to know if you will risk looking like a fool for love, for your dream, for the adventure of being alive . . . I want to know if you have touched the centre of your own sorrow, if you have been opened by life's betrayals or have become shrivelled and closed by fear of further pain! I want to know if you can sit down with pain, mine or your own, without moving to hide or fade it, or fix it. I want to know if you can be with JOY, mine or your own; if you can dance with wildness or let the ecstasy fill you to the tips of your fingers and toes. I want to know if you can disappoint another to be true to yourself; if you can bear the accusation of betrayal and not betray your own soul. I want to know if you can see beauty even

> when it is not pretty everyday; and if you can
> source your life on the edge of the lake and shout
> to the silver of the full moon YES!!!!!

How can churches become places that enable us to become more fully human?

First, by grasping the biblical rationale for this. The reason a church should seek to be fully human is that our humanness is what reflects God's likeness in us. The glory of God is seen in a human life—its sensuality, intellect, relationships, work, creativity, and worship lived to the full. To be fully human is to tie in with our original intention. To be redeemed is to be redeemed into all that we are meant to be; to be like Jesus, who is the most complete human being.

Second, by distinguishing between good and evil. By creating humans in the divine image, God endowed us an innate capacity for doing this. We can distinguish between good and evil by following an inner law that arouses the emotions appropriate to each: shame, fear, guilt are signs we re making wrong choices. Joy, resolution and confidence are signs we are making right choices. It is this innate capacity to distinguish between good and evil which we inherit from Adam. It is not Adam's sexual acts, but his example in making wrong choices, which turns us from good to evil.

Third, by revitalising the concept of Mother Church. There is an old Hebridean saying 'There is a mother's heart in the heart of God'. For the last decade of his life the Scotsman William Sharpe (1855–1905) wrote under the pseudonym of Fiona Macleod, perhaps thus reconnecting with his more feminine self. In his book *Iona*, published in 1910, he recalls this old Celtic prophecy:

> The Holy Spirit shall come again . . . All will be
> aware of the descending of the Divine Woman-
> hood upon the human heart as a universal spirit
> descending upon waiting souls.

Prophecy needs to be tested, and not all that comes from
Macleod's pen passes that test, but perhaps this prophecy does.

Robert Warren, the Church of England's Evangelism
Officer, has reminded many congregations that 'churches
should become the places, par excellence, where the general
public can find out how to live fully human lives'. A lady told
me: 'I don't want to go to a church that will judge me, but to
one that will understand me.' She will find a home in churches
that reflect the mother heart of God.

A former Elim pastor named Mark was reading Robert
Warren's book *Being Human: Being Church*. He was now
minister of a small independent fellowship. 'How do we
become a fully human church?' he asked.

We broke this huge challenge into four areas:

- Clear thinking about what it means from
  God's point of view (theology);
- Dismantling frameworks which inhibit this;
- Developing a lifestyle which expresses it.;
- Dealing with pitfalls which undermine it.

As Mark and I began discussing how a church can become
human he kept interjecting 'But our members would not go
along with that'. For example, they might assume that the way
to move into God's presence is 1980s style celebration; so to
have a time of worship in which there was no such singing, or
prophecy would be unthinkable. A stylised frame had replaced
being real together before God. So first, his church had to

dismantle a particular style which members associated with being fully Spirit-filled. Or they might plan a social occasion to which the public were invited, but because members felt driven to corner each non Christian and ask them to receive Jesus, the relish of the occasion and the spontaneity of friendship was lost. It became unnatural, and the guests never came again. So the stylised framework of evangelism had to be dismantled. His members had to be taught that Jesus built a relationship with people before he asked them to follow him.

Mark believes that a church of people who are becoming fully human connects with people at many places and levels, whereas old style approaches disconnect them. Thus his church hosts a harvest service that honours local businesses and education centres.

Households

> We have taken the major events of the home like birth, marriage and death, and have anaesthetised them by placing them in church.
>
> Archdeacon Martin Wallace

At first sight no two things have less in common than home life in biblical times and home life today. A Jewish or Celtic home was a long established, extended household around which the basic things of life revolved. A modern family has been described as a temporary arrangement of beds around a fridge and a micro oven; the important things happen elsewhere. Yet there is a golden thread that links the two: as the sparrow yearns to build a nest so does the human being

Jewish and Celtic models of the church in the home can spur modern Christians to exchange from artificial churchy duties for that of enjoying God together in their homes.

The Christianity of the Celts was a spirituality of the hearth before it was a spirituality of the church. Every household chore became a liturgy, because they practised ritually being present to God in each thing that they did. Thus familiar prayers for lighting the fire, dressing, cleaning, cooking, eating, welcoming visitors, retiring to bed became second nature. Births, marriages, deaths, anniversaries, homecomings were all celebrated in the home.

Contemporary household rituals are being well used. See, for example, volume three of *The Celtic Prayer Book*.[27] In some circles it is becoming fashionable to create prayer corners in homes. A work, study, eating or bed room may nowadays merge into an area of ikons, candles, prayer cards, Bible or tokens of creation that evoke adoration.

I believe many churches should release people from churchy duties which they are not really called to, and establish these two practices:

1. A weekly meal in households. During these each person is present to those who wish to tell of their 'journey' that week. A candle is lit, and prayer is offered. Friends who have no such household are invited to join them. A spare place is laid for Christ in the guise of the stranger or the unseen guest. This may take the form of the Jewish *Shabat* meal on Friday evenings, which Christians increasingly use.

2. A yearly blessing of the home with a celebration. Some people do this on St Brigid's Day, 1 February, and combine it with the custom of placing a Brigid Cross made of rushes in the home and extending this to store rooms, out-houses, caravans, boats which have been disused during the season of dark. Congregations which have adopted the cell model have a head start, but it is important that every member's home, where permission is given, is visited and blessed once a year.

Mystical and connected to the unseen world

> I am deeply convinced that great renewal will
> develop wherever communities enter regularly into
> solitude. Time for silence, individual study,
> personal prayer and meditation must be seen to be
> as important to all the members of the community
> as working together, playing together and worship-
> ping together. Without solitude we cannot ex-
> perience each other as different manifestations of a
> love that transcends us all.
>
> Henri Nouwen

'The biggest problem with evangelical Christianity' an evangelical pastor told me, 'is that they have to know all the answers. It robs them of so much.' Emerging churches foster windows of the soul, that is, the ability to read the signs of God's life in our everyday and inner worlds. This is spiritual literacy, heart knowledge, a way of awareness and seeing. *Spiritual Literacy: Reading the Sacred in Everyday Life* provides a stimulating anthology on this theme.[28]

In his letter to the church of Laodicia (Revelation 2) John urges the value of purity (white) and of inner seeing—churches need people whose eyes are washed in continual contemplation. Things that prevent this way of seeing in congregations are a worldview that dismisses the mystical and personal experience as worthless.

The deep need in the human soul for divine contemplation has long been repressed, but is now making itself felt. There is a mushrooming of prayer corners, prayer cells and poustinias in houses, gardens and monasteries.

How do church members who discover they are called to contemplative prayer stay in their church if it has no place for it? The vision of a cradle-in-the -making needs to be shared with their churches. Cradles are different from organisations.

> The greatest challenge to the church in the third
> millennium is to relate in a Christ-centred way to
> the Unseen World, which people on the Alter-
> native scene are far more at home with than are
> Christians.
>
> James Turnbull

Many of the most spiritual people believe in, visualise or
encounter spiritual beings. Yet Protestantism has said that the
things of heaven are unknowable. Second millennium churches
tended to ignore the biblical model of the Divine Assembly.
The writer of the book of Job depicts the Almighty as presiding
over an assembly of Divine offspring (Job 6). The second verse
of the Bible in Hebrew speaks of 'the Spirit Elohim' covering
the face of the earth. Exodus 19 describes Moses going up to
the Mount of the Elohim where one of the Elohim spoke to him.
El-lohim is a feminine word (El) with a masculine plural. It
means 'the divine beings or powers' at work in the human or in
the otherworld. The offspring of El were still active in New
Testament days; for example Gabri-El (Strength of El), Micha-
El (Likeness El). At Jesus' birth the angels praised El. And
Jesus is described as the Son of El (Immanu-El, Matthew 1:23)

The Bible also names God as The Most High. This makes us
aware that there is a hierarchy of beings, at the summit of which
is the Most High. Another biblical name for God is The Lord of
Hosts. There were a host of beings, earthly and heavenly which
constituted this host.

There are polarities within God: male and female (Genesis
1:27) light and darkness (Isaiah 45:7); Yahweh is both a warrior
and a mother (Isaiah 42:13,14)).

Ezekiel saw a vision of Yahweh in the form of four living
creatures representing the four fixed signs of Taurus, Aquarius,

Leo and Scorpio. Both models reappear in the last book of the Bible, the Apocalypse of St John, in the seven spirits of El Elyon and the four living creatures surrounding the throne of the Lamb (that is Christ, Rev 4:5) No aspect of creation is left out of the Divine Assembly. The cosmos was a unified organism, a macrocosm which is reflected in each individual who is a microcosm. There were planetary deities. Using a system that united the seven known planets of the day with the characteristics of the zodiacal signs the Sumerians had worked out the general patterns involved in each individual life. That need not detract from the freedom that is the birthright of each human being, and which Christ came to give back to us. To this day the motto of genuine astrology remains: 'The stars dispose but they do not determine'.

If gods and goddesses are seen for what they are, symbolic representations of created powers and energies, the raw material of cosmic life in all its diverse aspects, then they need to be valued in the light of their motivation. Often, in the Old Testament, prophets called believers to renounce false or evil gods; this was because they were in opposition to The Most High. In other passages God's spokesperson calls on them to bow down to The Most High, but not to disappear. The Greek version of Deuteronomy 32:43 bears this out:

> Rejoice with him, O heavens
> Bow down to him sons of God (that is Elohim,
>   sons of El)
> Rejoice with his people, nations
> Confirm him, all you angels of God.

Relationship and soul friends

'See how these Christians love one another' was a common saying in the first few centuries of the church. Since those times, those who wish to become members of the church have been required to accept a creed which states what they are to believe, but they have not been required to accept the Beatitudes (the beautiful attitudes commended by Jesus Matthew 5:1–12) which state how they are to relate. The emerging church puts the Beatitudes on a level with the creeds.

If the loving church is to replace the judgmental church, cells within the Body of Christ will have to learn new conditioned reflexes. Members of churches who visit Lindisfarne often ask 'How do we bring this about?' They want to serve Jesus, but do not want to do this in churches which are dominated by committees, clerics and conventions. I advise them to exercise faith. That is, to act as if relationship is primary in every conversation, committee and circumstance.

One church encourages any member who has upset another to take them a love gift the following day.

Equality of regard has become an accepted principle in our society. It was, for example, a building block of the 1998 Northern Ireland Good Friday Agreement. The emerging church has to be a community where this principle is practised.

At the heart of the doctrine of God is a communion of loving selves. In a book Italian theologian Bruno Forte describes the Trinity as 'a communion of flowing relationships'. We can only find our true identity as persons by reflecting this communion. As Charles Williams observed: it is as important to learn how we live from each other as how we are to live for each other.

In St Aidan's ancient kingdom of Northumbria there are still people, like him, who model church as friendship. When Rev Catherine Hooper, who had parishes in the Gateshead area, was killed in a car crash in 1999 a neighbour told The *Daily Telegraph*: 'It took her ages to walk to church because she was stopped by so many people along the way who wanted to talk to her. Before she came here very few people came to the church, but afterwards it was always packed, especially with young people.'[29]

People-friendly

> True evangelism always happens from within the culture. To adopt a new faith does not imply adopting a new culture.
>
> Martin Wallace

> The Christian faith never exists except as 'translated' into culture.
>
> David Bosch[30]

In the 1990s John Finney conducted research for the United Bible Societies in Britain on How People Find Faith. He summarised the findings in four words: 'Belonging comes before believing'. In USA George Hunter's research led him to a similar conclusion: More and more of the converts he questioned had felt that they were included and wanted in the church before they believed.[31]

Second millennium churches often thought it was necessary to crush all pre-and non-Christian spirituality for the sake of Jesus. It is true that if the church surrenders its soul to the spirit of the age it will have nothing to give, but it is equally true that if it fails to enter the soul of the people it will fail to give what it has. The Christian community has to be distinct from culture and yet immersed in it, as Jesus showed us.

Jesus was able to become one with the people in all things except sin because he remained one with the divine Spirit. That enabled him to lose earthly power, and became king of human hearts.

His critics, the Pharisees, had big evangelistic campaigns, but failed to turn round the hearts of the people. They imposed their culture, whereas Jesus stroked the people's culture. He took prime time to involve himself in their typical social gatherings (for example, a wedding at Cana John 2), religious gatherings (at synagogues) and occupations (for example, fishing). He gave himself to the poor, and did not put extra burdens upon them. He went to the most popular event of the year (Pentecost Festival Holiday), and illustrated his message with the most universally valued commodity—water. When Jesus made water taste like good wine (John 2) the need being met was a neighbourhood celebration whose swing was threatened—an extended family whose good name for hospitality was in the balance.

Some churches hedge round the Christian message as something 'unregenerate' people cannot understand. Jesus believed in freedom of information for all people. He held 'talkathons' in large open-air auditoriums (for example, Matthew 5–7). In order to baptise our culture we have to see it from the inside as God does. What is of God in it? How is God present in it?[32]

Emerging churches face the people. When someone took pot shots at one of her convents in a New York slum area Mother Teresa quietly went into the back yard, a tiny square of rubble and clothes lines, with an old, peeling statue of Mary, which faced the sisters while they worked in the kitchen. Mother Teresa stood there for a few minutes and then said. 'Turn the statue around. Let her face the people'. The sisters were never shot at again.[33]

Emerging churches 'befriend the chiefs'. The first evangelists in the British Isles had to persuade local rulers to open doors to them before any mission could begin. Postmodern society is becoming tribal again and the church must learn to relate to people groups. A Bishop advised a new young priest to 'target the tribal chiefs' in his local housing estate.

The police had lost control there, and a local mafia, who cruised the estate in expensive cars financed from drugs, took charge. They had a code which meant they 'looked after' the local community. When the vicarage was twice vandalised the new minister informed the local newspaper that they cared about the local community and were too poor to own the church house they lived in. On reading this the leader of the 'mafia' befriended the vicar, and promised to protect him and provide for the community. The 'mafia' provided a superb community fireworks display with cans of beer a-plenty. The debilitating cycle of dependency which marked other estates where the council ran everything was being broken; a community was being empowered in certain ways.

Emerging churches start from where local residents are. They follow the principle Do not try to teach anyone anything until you have learnt something from them. If we start where people are we will find that most people, even though they are unchurched, have a bank of spiritual experience upon which we may draw. God can and does speak to human beings because they are human beings, not because they are Christians. The Bible records many examples of this, none of which denies the necessity for witness.

The Alister Hardy Research Unit has discovered that nearly two thirds of the British population admits to having religious experiences, but that for a number of reasons people rarely talk about them. This includes children. Researchers such as David Hay[34] and Rebecca Nye conclude that for all children, not just those who have been taught religious beliefs, spirituality is an essential aspect of life.[35] They uncover three categories of spiritual sensitivity in children which they call awareness sensing, mystery sensing and value sensing. These make possible the exploration of spirituality in a broader context than the traditionally recognised languages.

Their findings suggest that children's natural 'relational consciousness' has been distorted or repressed by false constructs of Christianity. 'Value blockage' in Christian culture has been caused by factors which include the adoption of the Imperial mode by the church, which became an instrument of control; the assimilation by the church of dualistic Greek ideas; and the abdication by seventeenth-century theologians for defending spiritual awareness as a valid source of knowledge.[36]

My friend Liz Cannon, whose paper 'Children's Spirituality: An Unexpected Store' contributed to this research asks: 'Could it be that our secular culture is crushing the spirituality which is natural to children? Is it that at some level they discern that to be accepted in the secular culture of today, they have to let go of something which is very much part of them and integral to their life and wellbeing? And this crushing of children's natural integrated spirituality . . . even contributes to certain children's behaviour problems?' Retreating churches feared open exploration of spirituality, they exercised power by telling children what they 'ought' to hear rather than discovering God 'from whom every family on earth takes its name' (Ephesians 3:15).

Earth-friendly

> Christ's work is the ultimate reconciliation of all
> living creatures.
>> Karl Barth (Commentary on Colossians 1)

'My church teaches me to be reconciled with God and with people, but it does not teach me to be reconciled to the earth',

Catherine informed me. That could be said of most second millennium churches.

Many people seek a spirituality which is natural, and they feel violated if the church puts on unnatural airs, or neglects the earth.

Conservative twentieth-century churches rebuked those who claimed to find God in a garden. 'That is nature religion. It needs no Saviour', they said. The result was that people like William Hague, Britain's 1990s Conservative leader, declared that they went to church one Sunday a month, walked in the countryside the other Sundays, and gained more benefit from the latter.

Our pre-Christian forbears instinctively understood that the marriage of the human population with the fertile soil is necessary to the wellbeing of both. In the early myths of the Celts the god of the tribe mates with the goddess of the earth.[37] In the light of Christian revelation and modern science, that instinct can be seen as at heart sound. The early church, secure in its Jewish roots, understood this. God named the first man Earth (Adamah). Mr Earth's first act was to name, and thereby bless, each of earth's creatures (Genesis 2.7). In other words, the human being contains within themselves the whole earth. Jesus Christ, who St Paul names 'the second Adam' (1 Corinthians 15:47) comes from heaven, yet contains within his humanity the whole evolving earth story, and its groaning in anticipation of its coming total fulfilment (Romans 8:19–23)

Several centuries passed. Augustine taught that creation was an act of God's power. Celtic Christians saw that creation was an act of God's love. Maximus the Confessor (died 662) taught that the Creator-Logos has implanted in each created thing a characteristic 'thought' which is God's presence in and intention for it; this is its inner essence which makes it distinctively itself and at the same time draws it towards God.

By virtue of this indwelling logos each created thing is not just an object but a personal word addressed to us by the Creator. Thus the second Person of the Trinity acts as an all-embracing and unifying cosmic Presence.

The Celtic churches understood Christ, and therefore his Body, the church, as 'the bough' of creation. This way of seeing the creation drained away when bureaucratic ways came to dominate the minds and machinery of the Church.

The emerging church grasps this cosmic fullness of Jesus. It opens its doors to the whole earth community. The hundreds of thousands of people who, following the 'word' God has put within them to cherish the earth, but not knowing the story or the home of this 'word', will at last realise that creation is safe with Christians, and they will come home.

Earth, as a result of human action, is experiencing a monumental change. God is speaking to us through this. Our generation has been chosen by God to respond to the most momentous period of change in the billions of years of earth's history. The chemistry, bio-systems, geology and ozone layer are changing more radically than ever they have, and life systems are being extinguished at an unparalleled rate.

Creative arts

The emerging church walks hand in hand with the creative arts, because human creativity is a reflection of the Creator, though it must always cater for non-artistic people who value order more than experiment. The churches that have survived best provide a predictable framework which includes treasured, unchanging words and creeds, but they use these as a springboard for creativity, not as a straitjacket.

When Kim Erickson Haire worked as a waitress in various American cities, she became aware of a large group of people who were quite different from the people she met in churches.

She calls these 'the fluid people'. Fluid people, she observes, congregate at the vegetarian restaurant during Sunday lunch, while 'the Christians are institutionalised, singing words which originate on the surface of a page, skim the surface of their hearts, and echo off the surface of church walls'. She continues:

> Fluid people are liquid; they are poured into life and moving with the tide of the cosmos. They pour their spirits into art. Their souls feel somehow connected to the movement of the earth, and they search for meaning through colour, movement and harmony.
>
> Maybe the nerves somehow transfer differently to the brain, for this person actually feels colour; he flows with the shades, the depth and the richness; he becomes a part of its movement without form. She sees music, not as notes on a page, but as sounds which form movement in mirrors of light in her imagination, and if she is a praying person, she prays a dance to her God. He hears a rhythm that needs no music, it is the music of the earth, the strum of the wind, the gasp of the waves, the pulses of nature. She tastes the pain, the bitterness in the depth of a heart, or the sweetness which waits eagerly in the soul. He smells hope like expectant snow, clean and fresh; hope ready to burst through the cold greyness with brilliant crystals reflecting the true light of heaven . . .

Kim Haire concludes that most fluid people are consumed with the spiritual world, but few relate to Christ. She believes that the icon can be a powerful tool for disciplining the fluid person. The ikon, she writes:

has an intrigue which arouses the imagination and stimulates the senses of a person . . . it does not bend to the theatrical; it does not flaunt a gaudy Jesus on black velvet . . . The ikon reaches mysteriously from the cosmic realm into the human realm . . . To a believer, this truth is Christ—to the unbeliever it is a mystery, a mystery calling, urging, drawing the lost to seek and enter the kingdom of God.[38]

It is important that churches do not let the arts they use be divorced from the ever-fresh wells of creativity. In the stillness of dawn, fresh springs come to light.

Poets were part of the birthright of the biblical church.

The true poet is really a prophet. His gaze looks on things that others miss. It is no accident that in the original manuscripts, the words of the Old Testament prophets were written in poetic form.

Denny Gunnerson

The Welsh poet and Archbishop of Canterbury Rowan Williams describes the work of the poet as 'interpreting and harmonising the flow of the world's life in such a way that the shifts and changes of the world . . . can be unveiled as transfiguration, epiphanies of God's life'.[39]

Emerging churches weave poetry into their worship and also appoint bards.

Poetry leaves some people cold, and churches should be places where non-poetic people feel at home. These often respond to the good telling of a story. My journalist friend Clive Price met a member of a church in Denver, Colorado, which was founded by Indians. Clive told him what went on at a typical church meeting in Britain. 'Oh, we don't do anything like that' the church member replied, 'when we gather together we spend the time telling stories'.[40]

The retreating church either idolised or rejected signs and symbols. The emerging church, reflecting Christ's ministry, which overflowed with living symbols, celebrates the glory of God in painting and poetry, colour and sound, movement and music, symbol and drama. It brings colour back into the streets; it uses oil, water, fire, the earth and all its fruits. It seeks to rekindle a Christian imagination.

Roger Ellis of Revelation Church is giving himself to a church which is, in his words, emerging from the culture, not insulting it. He and Chris Seaton describe in their book *The New Celts* how God is leading them to establish culture friendly cafe churches for young people, and to use creative arts in worship:

> We have encouraged artists to come and draw what they feel is happening as the church worships together. We have also had sculptors and even potters working to one side of the meeting. Sometimes, in the process of the worship the artists are encouraged to interpret what it is they are portraying. At other times the work is left to stand in its own right and people are invited to go and view it at the end and ask the Holy Spirit to speak to them.[41]

In his book, *Which Way for the Church?*, the Reverend Doctor Rob Frost foresees a vital role for the arts in the church of the new millennium:

Music will take greater prominence and will become integral to the prayer experience. Prayer through music will be commonplace, be it sung Evensong, jazz mass, folk celebration or classic meditation.

The new churches will rediscover art, from the iconography of the East to the statues of Rome, and they will develop their own contemporary spirituality through it. Frequently changing displays, pictures, posters and banners will become a growing inspiration for prayer as the churches learn how to use the visual arts as a means and not an end . . .

In the new church drama will be seen as a prime means of effective communication. Actor Nigel Forte wrote 'Prophetic theatre is theatre which clarifies the word of God at a particular time; Evangelistic theatre is that which clarifies the Gospel in particular; Didactic theatre—in this context—clarifies the teaching of the Bible, and Entertaining theatre is based on the nature of human kind and creation . . .

The arts will not change or cheapen the gospel, nor will they replace preaching; they will complement it. The language of film, music, drama, poetry and dance will be the vernacular of the new generation, and the church will learn how to speak it, and speak it fluently.[42]

Unity and justice

During the second millennium three great strands of Christianity became separated: the Catholic strand of community around the Real Presence of Christ in the Eucharist;

the Protestant strand of personal conversion around the Bible; and the Orthodox (and in a sense the Pentecostal) strand of worship around an experience of the Holy Spirit. It was laid upon me that God wanted to weave these three strands together again, and that we were to let him weave them together in us as he willed.

Jesus said to his apostles: 'Whoever listens to you, listens to me'. The apostles were not always right, but they had been selected; they had responded, they spent time with Jesus. So we have to make an act of unity with the original apostles. I journeyed to the tombs in Rome in order to make an act of unity with Peter (a symbol of the Roman Catholic churches); with Paul (a symbol of Protestant churches, since he rebuked Peter for wrong behaviour); and I have subsequently made an act of unity with John (a symbol of the churches in Eastern and Celtic lands).

In his autobiographical book *Conjectures of a Guilty Bystander* (1966) Thomas Merton wrote:

> If I can unite in myself the thought and devotion of Eastern and Western Christendom, the Greek and the Latin Fathers, the Russian with the Spanish Mystics, I can prepare in myself the reunion of divided Christians . . . If we want to bring together what is divided we cannot do so by imposing one division upon another or absorbing one tradition into another. We must contain all the divided worlds in ourselves and transcend them in Christ.

In some deep and mysterious way, God was speaking also to me along these lines.

We have to make an act of unity with those God has placed in oversight in the churches today. There is disagreement as to how these leaders are meant to be appointed, but we all need to see that God has provided for our unity by giving us leaders. We should honour in the Lord all those who have been placed in oversight over churches which follow the orthodox Christian faith. This need not mean blind obedience—which in our plural society could not be the custom. But neither does it mean everyone does what is right in their own eyes. It means each of us should listen carefully, weigh thoughtfully, and communicate respectfully to other overseers.

Then we have to make an act of unity with God's Word in the Bible. Although Christians may have different understandings of the Bible, every Christian is required to approach it with deep humility, hungry to be fed, as a lover eagerly poring over a love letter from their beloved.

We have to make an act of unity with Jesus in Holy Communion. This sacrament means just that, Christians communing together with their Lord, visibly. Every time we receive the bread and wine we should make ourselves one with the whole Body of Christ on earth and in heaven, certain sections of the world church ban baptised members of other churches from receiving the bread and wine. This is on the grounds that they have broken away from the one church, and have therefore broken the biblical conditions for receiving Communion. Those who are excluded should adopt the attitude of the foreign woman who begged Jesus to give her some food, even if only the scraps left for the dog. Don't stay away; beg for scraps, which can take various forms according to local inspirations. Many churches, however, have an Open Table—it is open to all the beggars of the world who are hungry to be fed by Jesus. These Open Tables become powerful signs and experiences of unity, and emerging churches will have the spirit of The Open Table.

Strong leadership

> Good leaders grow people, bad leaders stunt them.
> Good leaders serve their followers, bad leaders
> enslave them.

Sir Adrian Cadbury
(Former head of Cadbury Schweppes)

Many local church leaders are dispirited by the mindset of their congregations. Postmodern churchgoers, one minister told me: 'think they'll come to church when it suits them, but they expect it to be there for them. The minister is reduced to a supermarket check-out attendant. The consumer mentality is killing both discipleship and the pastors. This mentality is an evil but few churchgoers recognise it as such. In the church it cannot be true that the customer is king: Jesus is King and we are to be the body that serves Him.'

How can they become inspired? They confuse loving people with meeting their expectations. When this confusion is aligned to a low self image it leads to disaster. Because they are not secure in their own identity in the God, these leaders become hostage to what is not of God in their people. In a study of effective leadership Des Dearlove poses the question why someone like Richard Branson, who failed school exams, can make a better leader than someone with a top university degree. His answer is that Branson's emotional intelligence, which Dearlove calls his 'people radar', is more keenly developed.

A new minister came to his church with an exciting agenda for change and development which he believed was from God. Various members opposed this or that item. His instinctive reaction was to regard them as enemies, and his flow of love towards them dried up. The members intuited that their minister did not love them for themselves, but only if they were fodder for his plans. The minister realised this. He decided that, instead of laying 'his stuff' on to his congregation, he would love them for themselves, and help to draw out what was of God in 'their stuff'. It was not long before the members realised that this was 'a new deal', and started to love him. That congregation is now a community.

This insight into leadership is validated by the American psychologist Daniel Goleman. In his groundbreaking book *Emotional Intelligence* he concludes that emotional rather than rational intelligence marks out the true leader. He claims that 'the very architecture of the brain gives feelings priority over thought'. Emerging church leaders know this.

The true servant leader is strong, not weak. A wise woman told me: 'What has departed from our culture is leaders who are strong, real. I am looking for leadership which is earthy, masculine, motherly and has a deep love which is reliable. An awful lot of godliness is up in the air. If you lean on it falls flat. Power corrupts. Absolute power corrupts absolutely.'

The Celtic church leaders had the physical courage to go out in front and vanquish monsters and evils. They did not play safe. They did not hide behind paper. Their humanity did not get squeezed out by the weight of topheavy committees. Their vulnerability did not get covered over because they operated in the safety zones of boards or old boy networks.

> Never trust a leader who walks without a limp.
>
> John Wimber
>
> The Abbot must so arrange everything that the strong have something to yearn for and the weak have nothing to run from.
>
> St Benedict

After St Cuthbert recovered from the plague he walked with a limp for the rest of his life. He was a strong leader, but I suspect this limp endeared him to the people.

The ability not to hide weakness is a mark of Christ-like leadership.

When large numbers joined the church in the first millennium it became a large organisation. It then required money from members to pay for clergy who did the most significant jobs. This marginalised the lay people. Soon the clergy became acclimatised to comfort and to the corridors and assumptions of power. They had no idea what it felt like to be homeless and powerless. All church leaders are prone to confuse their own ego with the will of God, and to impose the agenda of their own ego in the guise of religion.

Vulnerability is a voluntary relinquishment of the power to automatically protect oneself from being wounded.

This diagnosis of the retreating church is easy. But what to do about it? How can a large Body of Christ serve the masses and yet remain personal and sensitive to changing needs? In the Celtic model leadership was often given to those who renounced personal property and who were accountable another. Thus bishops were under the authority of a male or female leader of a monastery. In the emerging church people are led by those who have a Rule of Life which involves renunciation of power.

The early Celtic churches at their best managed to do two apparently opposite things. On the one hand they released Christians would wander off for the love of God, or work out their individual calling with the help of a soul friend. A bishop was given discretion to evangelise in any way that he felt was appropriate. He was a flying bishop, released from the burdens of church management, to move in mission wherever the Spirit led. On the other hand, the Celtic churches fostered communities and a sense of belonging. The abbot was a true father of a large family, a focus of unity, a sign of life-long stability to the many people who lived nearby.

In the emerging church the pastor sees her /his role as releasing people into being fully human. Celtic style bishops or trans-local church leaders come alongside congregations and bless what God is blessing. Anglican bishops still retain a faint residue of this way of operating; they spend year in mid-term visiting the people in and out of their churches, delegating, postponing or overlooking other duties.

Leaders in the emerging church are not afraid to use their intuition. They understand the soul of any venture. The soul of a venture is revealed in a crisis when facades are stripped away. Leaders define it; followers identify with it; the leader helps them to bond with it.[43] Leaders in the retreating church post-poned the painful decisions which were necessary to turn things round, for fear of the short term pain and controversy. Emerging church leaders grasp the nettle first of all, and then enjoy the fruits of peace and blessing. Leaders in the retreating church majored on minors; leaders in the emerging church major on major.

In the imperial model of the church leaders can be imposed by a hierarchy who are unknown, lack rapport with their people, and can therefore achieve little. The leaders of the Celtic Christian communities were the natural leaders of that people. This created problems when their heirs were less godly than those they led, but the system that replaced it of clergy being outsiders appointed by authorities that seemed alien was not the answer. Bishops in the early church, such as Martin of Tours and Cuthbert of Lindisfarne, were elected by the people. Popular technology now makes it possible for every church member in, say, a diocese, to vote for a candidate who they think should be considered.

In today's Celtic Orthodox Church a candidate for bishop is proposed and elected; he comes from the community. The introduction of local ordained ministers by other churches is a step in the right direction, but the system for assessing who should be ordained is class-ridden and myopic. In industry people are appointed according to their proven skills; the church still appoints people who pass paper exams but who lack rapport with people and leadership skills, and bypass many fine potential leaders who are neither called nor prepared to collude with a training system that is a travesty of true leadership.

Chapter 5

Fresh Shoots Downunder

There are a number of fresh expressions worldwide. We have three examples in this chapter; Urban Seed in Australia, Urban Vision in New Zealand and Ray's Community of Aidan and Hilda which is global. Other obvious examples here in Australia would be Urban Neighbours of Hope (UNOH), The Waiters Union, Cornerstone and Common Life to name a few.

Urban vision, New Zealand

Martin Robinson is a founding member of Urban Vision in New Zealand and has shared some of their story.

Not long ago a man in his early fifties in one of the high rises in my neighbourhood, began handing his wallet and possessions to some kids playing around on the eighth floor. Having emptied his pockets, he then climbed the concrete railing and jumped to his death. For this enclave of poverty and powerlessness—surrounded by so much wealth—this suicide was no new event.

Poverty is no new thing either, but from the mid-1980s, New Zealand became an international exemplar of free-market integration. And as has happened elsewhere, this served to create an increasing distinction between the winners and losers in this escalating game of unchecked acquisition. In this country, many of the poor in our neighbourhoods are represented in the worst statistics in the OECD. At the same time, when the church is successful, it is growing amongst the middle class. The poor are becoming increasingly marginalised, while the rest of society is becoming more ostentatious.

A response

> *Kotahi te koohao o te ngira e kuhuna ai te miro maa, te miro pango, te miro whero.*

Potatau Te Wherowhero

Officially formed in 1996, Urban Vision is a response to this growing injustice in Aotearoa. Each year we are free to choose to covenant to Urban Vision. We covenant to participate together in God's building of the Kingdom on the margins. We commit to:

- A year of deepening intimacy with Christ Jesus, our Lord and Saviour.
- Journeying with our Urban Vision community and *whanau* in increasing wholeness and integrity.
- Revealing God's loving justice amongst the poor and marginalised.

The *whakatauki* above by Potatau Te Wherowhero, tells us that three different coloured threads will go through the eye of one needle. For us this means our inward journey, our communal journey and external focus are all tied up in the heart of God.

We currently have forty-two adult members (twelve of whom are trialling with particular teams) and twenty-one children in six specific contextual apostolic communities. Five of these communities are sited in urban poor and marginalised neighbourhoods. In Wellington City we have three communities—Mt Cook, Newtown and Newtown Park. Twenty minutes drive from the city there is a newly formed community in Cannons Creek, Porirua. Some eight hours of driving away, there is a team in Merivale, the poorest part of Tauranga. Our sixth centre is an hour's drive from Wellington up the Kapiti coast, at Ngatiawa, in the foothills of the brooding Tararua Ranges. This is intended as a home for each team, a rural retreat from the city, representing the sense of action/reflection that we aspire to.

Our membership has fluctuated hugely in recent years, but now we are pruned and ready for sustainable growth. We are certainly not wanting to become large, but do want to catalyse other movements where possible. Three of our six communities are less than a year old—the other three are reasonably strong and are resourcing themselves for a more sustainable future in their particular contexts. We have greater clarity in our structures and a far stronger sense of common understanding than we have ever had. Now that we have passed our first decade of existence, we are addressing our sustainability more thoroughly.

Beginnings

Urban Vision officially began in 1996, but its roots extend further back into old friendships, shared schooling and common ministry. Justin and Jenny Duckworth were running youth ministries in Berhampore, a suburb of Wellington City, with Youth for Christ (YFC). Martin and Alison Robinson, and Nick and Phillippa Young were sharing a flat in the same suburb and were working with refugee and migrants from the Horn of Africa. Alison, Jenny and Nick were old school and church friends, Phillippa and Alison are sisters, Justin and Martin ran and studied theology together. We all had a shared missional commitment, with a conviction that travelling together is more encouraging and a more powerful witness to God's love.

What's in a name?

Together with other YFC people in Berhampore, we all decided to choose a name for our intentional community in 1996. In the end, we each compromised with 'Urban Vision'—it was nobody's first choice (but then 'kenosis oasis' may have rhymed and had a thrilling theological ring to it, but it sounded silly). The idea behind the name is the belief that we all wanted to participate in the revelation and establishment of God's kingdom amongst the poor and marginalised in urban areas—this belief remains.

Increasing clarity and maturity

In our earlier years we were closer to a purely anarchist movement—intent on telling others about their shortcomings and weaknesses. While there were some vibrant ministries amongst young people and refugees, a good proportion of us were also known as 'rent a crowd' for any action, demonstration or vigil that was on offer. Some received police harassment for burning Indonesian flags or protesting outside the Indonesian Embassy about East Timor. Others received church harassment for not doing things the 'proper' way. We still contend that being radical is actually more orthodox than much that is palmed off as orthodoxy.

We still very much embrace that prophetic element, confronting and unmasking the powers, but we generally see this as more contextually linked than we did. For instance, instead of unilaterally choosing issues of injustice and being involved in any protests and actions, we now will usually only be involved in actions that spring from the people we are in solidarity within our communities. The emphasis is on the needs of our neighbourhoods.

Finding our own way

In 1999, we had an amicable split from YFC. This was in full recognition that the life we had developed went way beyond the usual fare of YFC. It was time to develop this further without having to deal with a YFC structure developed for other purposes, leaving YFC free to develop in its own way.

By this stage we were connected to a range of churches and denominations: Catholic, Presbyterian, Orthodox, Baptist, charismatic and Pentecostal. The irony was that we had no Anglican connections at that point. Now, many of us are connected to Anglican churches in our given locality.

Increasingly, we came back to define our core charism, which was to be Jesus-centred contextually focused sustainable communities, sent to love and work with the poor and marginalised in Aotearoa/New Zealand.

Our membership has fluctuated over the years. Now that we have raised the discipleship bar somewhat, our membership has become more mature and has a lot to offer their neighbourhood and any church they may be associated with. This has also served to clarify what we are about, and be free to say what we are not.

Bicultural Journey

New Zealand's constitutional foundations begin with the Treaty of Waitangi in 1840. It was to be a document promising a foundation of justice and equity between the English Crown and *tangata whenua* (the people of the land). In subsequent decades, the New Zealand government and many Maori, broke faith with the treaty. Huge injustices were perpetrated and legislated.

By the 1970s, a significant groundswell had developed both inside and outside the church to deal with these injustices. As a result, *Pakeha* (white) Christians are having to come to terms with the Treaty and develop a truly contextual spirituality, rather than simply copying British or American activities and perspectives. For us in Urban Vision, this has meant the need for greater engagement with Maori perspectives and customs, and an intentional working towards reconciliation. It has meant the inevitable engagement with the fruits of discrimination and injustice (both personal and systemic) in this country which have left Maori overly represented in every negative national statistic. For instance, many of us have protested and/or been on parliamentary vigils on issues of racial injustice. Many have taken part in *Hikoi* (protest walks). We are currently developing an indigenous sacred calendar that dovetails with the Anglican Church's existing one. For instance, we have developed a prototype annual Parihaka memorial service which remembers the West's first ever confrontation with non-violent Christian protest—when the New Zealand government invaded Te Whiti and Tohu's peaceful community at Parihaka in 1881.

Within Urban Vision, we have a majority of Pakeha, and an influential small group of Maori. Some of us are immersing ourselves in Maori language and culture either because our specific missional context demands it, as well as realising that it is important to know our indigenous language. All of our children (twenty-one of them and growing) are developing a bicultural identity in school, community and Urban Vision contexts.

For those of us who are of European extraction, calling ourselves 'Pakeha' (white) instead of 'European' immediately acknowledges our bicultural commitment. On a practical level, Urban Vision has an annual *Hui* (full gathering) on a nearby *Marae* (the ancestral home and gathering point of an Iwi or clan). On the *Marae* a Christian *Kaumatua* (wise elder) has embraced us and encouraged our faltering journey. Within

Urban Vision we all use Maori language to a greater or lesser extent. Some are actively working out a specific Maori contextual approach to their community (for example, the Cameron family in Tauranga). None of us can turn away from the necessity of engaging with what it means to pursue a bicultural journey with integrity.

We continue to learn so much from our Maori brethren, about the importance of holistic spirituality that incorporates a deep sense of community and responsibility for the planet (similar to Celtic spirituality). We are also challenged in the way we apply Western missional models which seem to be highly influenced by urban dislocation perspectives, rather then the imperatives of sustainability and becoming people with a long-term presence and environmental responsibility. While we will continue to learn from and dialogue with western Christian models and practices, we have learnt to discern the weaknesses of paternalistic and modernist models from overseas and we try to take account of an indigenous worldview.

Highlights

We have had many highlights over the years. Doing life together is such a rich experience. Oh the things we have done. The pains we have shared. The tragedies endured.

Some wonderful highlights have been: the pioneering and sustaining of many life-giving ministries such as the Newtown film club with mental health consumers, community film competitions, community development amongst numerous communities both indigenous and refugee/migrant, the Ngatiawa Rural Retreat Centre, our bicultural journey (Maori and Pakeha (New Zealand European) learning to walk together in greater wholeness and justice), increasing ecological focus linked to local and worldwide issues of injustice, vast creative resources and inspiration within our wider communities and ludicrously successful community musicals.

Key challenges

At this stage some of our key challenges are:

Taking our bicultural journey further
What should it look like and where are we headed?

Movement versus contextual autonomy
In the last few years this has served to be a significant issue, and we lost one of our key ministries over it. We are trying to balance our strong desire for deep contextual autonomy with travelling together as a movement of the like-minded. But to travel together, there does need to be agreement.

When you have mostly recruited from amongst the anarchic, highly postmodern fringes of the church, you are likely to get phobic reactions to words like 'leadership' and 'submission'. In fact, in the New Zealand psyche, these words have become emotionally (and unnecessarily) welded to a feeling of subjugation or being the victim. Many of us in our movement have done a lot of personal counselling work to move to greater wholeness and freedom in this. We no longer need to be so inherently reactionary or cynical, but more embracing of the differences and gifts people offer to the whole, and the need at crucial times to sacrifice personal ambition for the communal good. This is a very foreign concept in a western world captivated by the cult of the individual. We have learnt a lot about community from our Maori brethren in this regard.

Sustainability
In recent years we have seen that this issue is closely linked to leadership. We were too hasty in earlier years to move on from

ministries recently set up, when a sustainable lifestyle had clearly not been imbibed, and leadership was clearly floundering. We are now working at building centres of culture within our movement that are well resourced and serve to champion sustainable lifestyle for all those who are new and helping any new teams that are setting up.

To be or not be an order

We are looking at whether we become more closely linked to the Anglican denomination and maybe become an order. The fun-loving, low-commitment, entertainment-driven prevailing church culture is quite at odds with where we are currently. We are more than a para-church because of our emphasis on community and development of spiritual rhythms. To all intents and purposes, we are an order. But to formally become one—will that unnecessarily impede those who might have explored us otherwise (for example, Carey's Serempore Brotherhood was an order by another name)? Would becoming an order marginalise us further, or give us the sense of clarity we need to move ahead more effectively?

While there is a sense of agreement amongst much of Urban Vision that an order could be the way to go, do we stay non-denominational or choose a denomination? While some of us believe denominations are dying, many of us are sensing the need to be formally connected with a denomination, but which one? Many of us have strong historical connections with a range of denominations—how will closer links with one be viewed by other denominations?

Part of our issue also is the steady aging and maturing of Urban Vision. We are increasingly becoming a missional community of 'marrieds with children'. For the first time in our history, we are starting to attract 'marrieds with children'. While this gives us a sense of stability in some ways, it can make some teams less enticing to risk-taking singles. We need to carefully discern the way ahead.

Urban Seed, Melbourne

In 1987 Collins St Baptist Church (CSBC) asked what does it mean to be church in the unique neighbourhood of the city centre. Guided by the long and careful work of the Reverend Ron Ham, the church began to explore themes of regeneration and urban mission, seeking the ideas of those such as the Reverend Tim Costello, from an inner-city church in St Kilda. In 1990 CSBC appointed Reverend Jim Barr to come and further develop the church's response to urban mission. In 1993, closely supported by Ron Ham and Peter Chapman from the nearby City Life mission, Jim took the initiative of establishing what was then called the Urban Mission Unit (now Urban Seed, <www.urbanseed.org>).

The initial ideas for the work of Urban Seed began with a professional and academic approach to mission. It was envisaged that Urban Seed would conduct research and training with a focus on Australian culture and urban spirituality. Some of the important work established during this time were the Seeds Program of discipleship formation, city walks and experiential mission exposures.

The residential community at Central House was established in 1995 when three interns moved into the old Collins Street Baptist Church property officers' residence on Level 9. This development would come to play the major part in the development of the practice and ethos of Urban Seed. In the same year, Tim Costello was appointed as the new Director of Urban Seed, which was another critical factor in the evolving character of Urban Seed's work.

The first internship was constructed around the ideas of a 'monastic' rhythm of life of twelve hours in mission, twelve hours studying (SEEDS and external tertiary) and twelve hours work doing property duties around the church for a small salary each week. Inspired by the example of Peter Chapman's seventeen-year ministry through 'City Life' at the Presbyterian church next door, these first interns spent much of their time walking the streets of Melbourne meeting people. After three months they invited friends they had made to join them in their house for lunch. This formed the basis of the spiritual discipline of the community's open lunchtime which has run ever since and which is currently held in the 'Credo Café'.

Over the coming years interns joined with Tim Costello in proclaiming and helping others to discern the spiritual nature of the city through walks and public speaking. Out of this discernment a prayer vigil of public witness and protest was organised outside the then recently opened Crown Casino. These were the early attempts of the community to breathe new life into an old and proud tradition of public engagement of Collins Street Baptist Church.

Between 1995 and 2006 fifty-four people have come to live at Central House, and each year the intake of residents built upon these early initiatives. Since 1995 much has developed within the residential community, and yet many of the early elements remain the same:

- relational presence in the inner city
- the discipline of hospitality, sharing meals and living space in the church
- home with those considered least
- discernment walks and public speaking
- public liturgy and protest
- exploring Christian community
- balancing work, study and mission
- common work in and around the building

In 1999 Urban Seed and the residential community decided to understand and organise itself around four themes that had emerged from its history. These were Spirituality, Mission, Community, and Learning. These four elements form a 'rule' that directs the life and rhythm of the community. It aims to create space to help the community to reflect theologically and maintain its focus in the movement toward Christ. Each of these four elements is thought about through stories which are important to the community.

In late 2001, the Urban Mission Unit became Urban Seed. The name 'Urban Seed' holds the organic work of building community in tension with the concrete context of urban life. It stems from the conviction that the things that really give life in this world must be grown. The work of making meaningful connections between people, restoring relationships of love and justice, caring for the earth, and discovering spiritual life, all require nurture. None of these things can be imposed or artificially generated.

This history has been shaped by many extremely gifted people. The one thing that has been a standout charism for Urban Seed has been the willingness to engage. This has come through primarily a commitment to neighbourhood in the midst of the inner city extremes of wealth and poverty. On any given day at Credo Café, these extremes of society, with everything in between, will be represented in some way. We mostly attract marginalised people because lunch is free; however it is a high priority to keep it 'open' to all.

The commitment to engagement has meant trying to stay connected to inherited churches. It's easier for groups to write the inherited church off all together and form new 'emerging' churches. It has often been a bumpy ride, but Urban Seed and Collins Street Baptist Church (CSBC) have a relationship. Urban Seed has been the breath of new life in the nine-storey building that is 'Central House', attracting creative people to explore ways of holistic ministry.

Some of the tensions have existed because of process. Urban Seed has a flat structure and is somewhat anarchistic, where as CSBC have a traditional Baptist understanding of a diaconate. When running an organisation like Urban Seed it is not always easy to have decisions going through unpaid, although highly committed deacons who meet together semi-regularly. This was a factor for Urban Seed having to find its own relatively independent identity.

Living issues have also come up when sharing a building. In 2000 we had twelve residents living at 'Central House' at the peak of Melbourne's heroin crisis. Our back laneway became the most frequented area in the CBD for injecting drug use. We were constantly responding to overdoses as a team and realised that we were actually keeping people alive, people who may have otherwise fatally overdosed in places where no one was present.

As well as keeping people alive, we could offer refuge and friendship in Credo Café. This helped greatly with overcoming people's feeling of marginalisation. For some in the church it was seen as a way of encouraging drug use and basic arguments of harm minimisation and the best approach for injecting drug user's health and wellbeing were often debated. For us, the 'non-professional' (which does not make it unprofessional) approach we adopt of offering friendship first and foremost was what was needed for a majority of these 'outcasts'.

Living at your place of mission and worship gives rise to the images of the 'Celtic' style monasteries that we have explored in earlier chapters. We have always attracted great people to Urban Seed and the dilemma has been just what these people can do when their internship in the city has finished. A small number of Seeders, particularly after our incorporation, have been able to create jobs to stay in the city and stay connected. This has come through money from philanthropic and corporate engagement and also sustaining a business of schools seminar and walks which Chris Lacey has worked particularly hard on.

We've found that corporates and philanthropists are really keen to fund our work. They understand and like our 'community development' model which we would call church. The idea of 'thick' and 'thin' language has often been debated at Urban Seed. In order engage the world, we have found it useful to find language that people understand. Often people are invited in by this non-religious 'thin' language we use such as 'community development'. Credo Café to outsiders is a unique chance to build relationships with marginalised people and also wealthy corporates in Melbourne's CBD. However our 'thick' theological language says that is communion with people as diverse as 'tax collectors' and 'notorious sinners' exploring the journey of discipleship.

Our tensions

Our tension with 'thick' and 'thin' language and the need to broaden our base so that people have communities to go to was some of the reason for taking the Seeds program in whole new direction. Seeds allows us to use 'thick' language, which we know is needed to sustain the activism of Urban Seed as evidenced on the Seeds website (<www.seeds.org.au>).

Our idea is to run Seeds as 'new monastic' missional communities, that can have Urban Seed as a funding base for DGR (Deductible Gift Recipient) status with work done in the alleviation of poverty. Urban Seed can remain as a 'public' front for Seeds communities beyond the city that allow us to engage in non-threatening ways. We have explored this with Norlane in Geelong and also in Bendigo and Footscray. We hope to align with the Baptist Union, yet remain ecumenical, just as UNOH (Urban Neighbours of Hope) have managed to do with the Churches of Christ. There is less commitment required to be connected with Seeds than there is with groups like UNOH. Less commitment will have its pitfalls I'm sure, just as high commitment can also have pitfalls with the amount of people who can be committed to fairly 'strict' rules.

Beyond the city
Norlane is probably further down the track than the other areas. The Norlane Baptist Church was once a thriving place. However like many other churches it has been in rapid decline for many years. The Baptist Union were pretty close to shutting it down and so we had the opportunity to try and resurrect something using the great facilities. The Baptist Union of Victoria (BUV) has been supportive of the slow nature of rebuilding. As a long-term resident of Geelong, travelling to Melbourne daily for work, I realised that I needed to be enacting something of Urban Seed's ethos in my own neighbourhood. This was the right opportunity. My wife Belinda and I, along with a few other Urban Seeders, decided to incarnate into Norlane, Geelong's poorest suburb and get to know the neighbours using some Urban Seed principles.

I've become the Norlane Baptist 'Minister' by default really, even though this is a Seeds/Urban Seed thing. It is helpful in the local community to be able to say use terms that people are familiar with like Baptist Church and Minister. People would struggle with 'I'm the Seeds Convener for Geelong' I think. It's also a nice way to keep connected to the inherited church. It's also acknowledges that the Norlane Baptist Church has gathered on this site for over sixty years.

Because we don't constitutionally exist as a church with the Baptist Union, we have come under the 'New Missional Community' banner with the BUV. This is a learning experience for the denomination as well as the new communities that are coming in to being. This may allow us to have people committed more to a rule or an annual covenant rather than straight out church membership.

Each Monday more than forty locals gather for a Credo style sit-down meal that isn't just a soup kitchen. We all eat together and take the opportunity to build genuine relationships. We call the café area 'The Longroom' because it is a long room with a long communal table. (The irony wasn't lost on the local folk as being reminiscent of establishments such the Marylebone and Melbourne Cricket Clubs!) We also have a Friday open lunch which is less busy.

One important aspect of our meal is that we haven't tried to do it in isolation. There are a number of different partnerships involved. Our partnership with the 'Uniting Care' emergency food relief agency in our neighbourhood is extremely important. The local volunteers may not always understand the principle of a community meal as opposed to a welfare-providing soup kitchen (everyone likes to be 'helpful' and 'useful'). However, the partnerships keep us accountable, and help us to continually examine our own principles. This helps to maintain the idea that this isn't just a franchise of Urban Seed.

We have Mark Pierson inspired gatherings on Sunday mornings, which are very low key and easy to run. The same layout for a service is used most weeks and it is participatory. We have three young people living out of some rooms that we made in the back of the chapel. It captures the nature of Celtic monasteries by opening up a space that can retain a sense of the sacred as well as being public.

Marcus' thoughts on Seeds

Marcus Curnow is our 'Bard' and has been working really hard to name exactly what a Seeds community might look like. He describes Seeds as a way of being church that is based upon an understanding of a shared conversation, connections and commitments.

It's a fluid and anarchic sense of church where creative, earthy and accessible public worship gatherings are valued as important but are ultimately seen as secondary. Our worship gatherings arise only out of the more essential practice of a robust local word, household and table based spirituality that empowers people in practical, lifestyle oriented mission initiatives.

In a society in which our sense of home is fragmented, made fragile or commodified, we see our spiritual search as a struggle to 'Grow Home.' Seeds is emerging as a covenant between local communities from various places in order to provide an economy of common life and connection necessary to continue the work of growing home. Seeds Covenanted Communities (or what we colloquially call 'Seedy Mobs') are a Christian response to the homelessness (spiritual, economic, political and social) that many of us experience.

From our Urban Seed experience, three key elements emerged for Seeds Covenanted Communities.

Know the Word

We seek to know and be known by God's message of truth, love and justice by gathering together to pray, discern and celebrate our participation in the living story of Jesus Christ. It includes our 'slow' approach to worship gatherings, bible study, and public missional conversations such as city walks and seminar series. Being 'ecumenical' we encourage our punters to share and discover how the distinctive paths of each others different spiritual journeys and traditions can inform our own. One way we have done this is by reframing the great Aussie tradition of the 'pub crawl' with 'church crawls' through Melbourne's CBD where we spend fifteen minutes on Sunday in each church, getting a smorgasbord taste of the different traditions.

One of the distinctives of Seeds has been our approach to the biblical text through creative studies, prayerful reading and discernment walking. Indigenous Australians have a concept of 'songlines' which involves telling stories in order to navigate through the often difficult Australian landscape. The stories form a key part of cultural identity and memory and often act as codes for articulating tribal boundaries and key pointers for survival along the way. Inspired by such ideas we have sought to use our own sacred stories as a map by which we walk around our neighbourhoods and view reality. This improvisational, narrative and public approach to spiritual life, seeks to find ways for the biblical story to wash with our personal stories and the larger narratives of the world in which we live.

Many times during street based bible walks I have seen peoples eyes opened as they start to see their 'everyday' through gospels categories. Many biblical texts point to the 'song' and 'voice' of creation and Jesus himself suggested if his followers didn't cry out in worship the stones themselves would do so. On our walks we take time to listen. Sometimes it's the unexpected interruptions from rich and poor alike that make it feel like we are living a gospel story as the Word on the street is literally made flesh amongst us. What started in the city as a personal spirituality experience is now conducted with thousands of people from churches, school students and business people each year and is a key aspect of our mission engagement.

Using the teaching tradition of Jesus we ask a lot of open ended and rhetorical questions on such walks. Questions have a power to animate a diversity of responses and have been a key aspect of our spirituality. In discerning the Word we have been influenced by the Quaker's adoption of testimonies, queries and advices which have sustained a non-hierarchical and non-doctrinal based movement of Christian community and activism.

Grow home

We seek to grow a new sense of home in local places by re-discovering and re-imagining the traditional vows of poverty, chastity and obedience. This has been inspired for us by Ched Myers useful evaluation of the radical discipleship movement (*Who Will Roll Away the Stone*, Orbis, 1994). Seeds has been indebted to and emerged out of Melbourne's strong tradition of experimental Christian communities many of which arose and fell based upon close ties to the 1960–70s counterculture. Myers suggests the need to draw on more ancient sources, particularly the so called 'evangelical vows' which have sustained Christian households in 'growing home' alternatives across many ages and places.

For us the vow of poverty is not about being poor or idealising poverty, it is however about seeking to live simply. It implies a deepening solidarity with those who are marginalised by poverty which we prioritise by moving into poorer neighbourhoods so we can see and serve the world from this perspective. Because the vow should actually point to the ultimate alleviation of poverty we commit to economic sharing. For us the perceived difficulty and pain of attempting a common purse has taken a back seat to a culture of inspiring each other to keep taking constant steps both big and small. Our queries and advices suggest renewable household covenants around aspects of economic life like sharing time, energy, work and money, processes of food and green living.

For Seeds the essence of the vow of chastity is seen as honouring the sacred connections between God, creation and each other's bodies. As such it has been less about sex and more about food. Whilst sex is often an issue for community so is the price of vegetables! We can live without sex but not food! Many of our discernment queries around chastity challenge us to explore the simple but profound connections that can be made by making the production and consumption of food central to our spiritual life. Eating 'slow' food around an open table helps create a sense of shared community and often reframes the life giving power of the Eucharist for us.

The vow of obedience is difficult for power literate, post-colonial educated, Australian's who have also been socialised by consumer capitalism. Much of the 'Seeds' branding is about capturing the sense of the anti-power of being small and uncontrollably organic. Whilst seeking to encourage the gift of leadership among us we have generally maintained small groups and flat structures inspired by Dave and Angie Andrews and Waiters Union in Brisbane. In a highly individualised world we consider 'obediences' as being faithful to the mutual decisions we make to live this vision with others even if we don't always win or don't always agree. Even in disagreement we choose to unite around the ongoing conversation and the questions and covenant to each other on a yearly basis.

Interestingly the non-violence tradition with its Sermon on the Mount inspired literacy about power and Christianity is shaping many of our queries about obedience as we seek to learn the arts of mutual submission. It regards Jesus' active and militant non-violence as a necessary discipleship discipline against evil power structures and has seen the development of Seeds obedience queries around the practice of civil disobedience.

Go engage

We seek to serve others through re-discovering and re-imagining the missionary instructions of Jesus to teach, heal and cast out evil (Mark 6). Such practices are understood quite differently in the various Christian traditions from which we come but we find these more helpful than secular social science or welfare categories in keeping us united in our activism and keeping it connected with our spirituality. Our queries and advices call us to critically return to the stories of Jesus when considering any new mission model, program or idea.

In the heart of the Melbourne we have expressed these three instructions through ministries of education, hospitality and political advocacy respectively but they look and feel quite different in different places and in the lives of our punters. It is in the general mix of these missional aspects rather than the emphasis of one over another that we get a sense of the breadth of God's own mission and also experience the necessity of a community approach which share's the vocational strengths as well as provides the necessary corrective for the weakness and missional biases that can arise from our unique personalities, upbringings and faith traditions.

Expanding on 'growing home'

Having arisen out of walking alongside people experiencing dislocation and homelessness the theme of *home* is central to understanding and practicing this charism. As we 'seed' in a neighbourhood, we look for signs that God has taken on flesh and 'moved into the neighbourhood' in Jesus, reconciling people with each other, with God, and with Creation. Our way of life is to co-operate with the work that Jesus is doing, and to model our way of life on the Jesus we see in the Gospels. As a seed brings life by falling into the ground and dying, so we hope to bring life by incarnating into the lives of poor neighbourhoods.

To grow home we recognise we need an ongoing process of reconciliation with God, ourselves, other peoples and the earth. Only communities that prioritise this necessity will work. Growing home is an organic process of life and death; strength and weakness. The weakness of the seed is also its power.

We do not grow home in our own strength, but through the gracious hospitality of God in the incarnation, life, death and resurrection of Jesus Christ. In light of this grace we seek to make our homes places of hospitality and make ourselves dependent upon the hospitality of those we would seek to serve. This concept of home can be more public than an individual household and may look more like a 'monastery' with people eating and living together as at Credo Café in Melbourne and the Longroom in Norlane.

Our use of the term 'mob' was inspired by Mark Brett, a Hebrew Bible scholar who has done much work of solidarity and listening to the faith and cultural experience of Indigenous Australians. When Indigenous Australians meet, the question of 'Who is your mob?' is often the first question asked. This is reminiscent of Jesus' 'Who is my mob?' question in Mark 3: 31–3. It is a concept that includes a sense of extended family, relationship with and responsibilities for particular land, place, stories, totems and 'songlines' which define social relationships. At a time when we were looking for more positive categories to describe our understanding of church he encouraged us to explore the connections between biblical ideas of 'church' and that of Indigenous tribal groups.

Now there can be problems when powerful non-indigenous people adopt such a term. It can be an idealistic projection; a dishonest co-opting of language of which we have little real experience. For us it remains a reminder of what we have humbly learned from the indigenous people we have met on our journey. It express something of the ongoing struggle for reconciliation and the desire for a gospel and church that is truly indigenous to the Australian landscape.

The slow movement

An important part of growing home is the idea of 'slow food'. It's pretty easy to eat poorly in the fast food culture of Melbourne's Central City. The overworked corporate grabbing a burger on the run often bumps into the underemployed beggar coming in the door united by the temptation of sugar, salt, and fat. It's a meal of convenience that feels okay while you're eating it but does little to satisfy and long term makes you fat, lazy and sick.

As 'mobs' we seek to create an alternative food culture by establishing a worshiping missional community around the production and consumption of a meal which is inclusively offered to homeless people and corporates alike in Credo Cafe, where you can 'taste and see' some different values. This is modelled in our other Seeds table gatherings as well.

Some of the different values of these meals take their cues from the slow food movement which arose in Italy as a response to the negative impact of multinational food companies and is spreading around the world—slowly! Slow food opposes the standardisation of taste, protects cultural identity tied to food and seeks to safeguard traditional processing techniques. It involves valuing time to prepare, eat and build community through food. It is sometimes critiqued as being an upper class pursuit, however far from extravagant eating, slow food is about the celebration of the connections that food can make with sustainable production and local food traditions that are often lost in the dominant economy.

Slow worship

The slow food movement has helped us reframe our understanding of what it means to be 'church'. It has been said that if you read the gospels without getting hungry you aren't really paying attention. The how, what, where and with whom Jesus eats is a central point of gospel conflict and, coming out of the feeding miracles, 'understanding about the loaves' (Mark 6:52) is presented as essential to understanding Jesus' ministry of reconciliation.

After a decade of sharing lunch with homeless people we have decided we want to explore a slow worship movement. This has little to do with singing slower or less songs (although this has been a useful result!). Rather than just picking up a pre-packaged worship meal it's been about reflecting on what we are wanting to do/achieve in worship and taking time, in our local setting, to use local resources that reflect our local community culture. Firstly our worship is slow because it has taken a long time to come about. It is worship that has come out of a sense of mission.

The first Urban Seed worship gathering was a prayer time before lunch at Credo Café. As homeless people started assisting with meal preparation the nature of the prayers changed and the meal itself became a kind of sacrament. Lots of our prayers, songs and interactive style have come from this dynamic. Our slow worship is often improvisation that has come from a core of people who have been bonded through the shared experience of difficult mission and only after a decade of being the church on everyday except Sundays.

Slow food looks at the connections between consumption and production and this is also vital for our worship. Some of the principles that Mark Pierson shaped up at the beginning of these gatherings included a commitment to good consumption where the emphasis is upon creating spiritual desire rather than just meeting spiritual needs. So much of our church culture seems to be about meeting needs.

We would suggest that Jesus teaching methods were more about creating spiritual desire than meeting spiritual needs. Desire and need are connected. Much of negative consumer culture is about the production of a false consumer desire which redefines wants into felt needs. The response in John 6 of the disciples who stay on with Jesus after his feeding controversy ('Where else will we go?'), says something of worship and necessity. The only communities that work are those of necessity; we all need to eat—physically and spiritually—and so we would seek to base our worship around peoples' deepest needs by replacing the ancient Hebrew 'Bread of the Presence' and the Eucharist love feast at the heart of our liturgy

Mark Pierson has inspired us through his 'Slow Food and Worship Seminars'. He suggests what people are longing for in worship is breadth and depth. Our 'Dead Man Waiting' Easter Saturday service in 2006 was attacked by the Sydney Anglicans as being superficial. The critique is that alternative worship prioritises image over words and style over substance. As if a church service containing 125 kilos of ice would somehow water down the Gospel!

Actually the service was far from superficial but based around the psychological stages of grieving (including denial, anger, guilt/shame/self-blame). Some people would not have realised the depth of this framework shaping the event in any conscious way however the substance of this allowed space for people to grieve their lives. It was very powerful for many

Christians who had not considered these themes at depth and also for non-churched people who appreciated the non-threatening invitation to explore very threatening themes!

Breadth includes ranges of peoples and backgrounds, stages of faith, good explanations and intros or worship elements, a variety of learning styles, a balance of traditions and repetitions with new forms and ideas. It sees worship within broader contexts of justice, politics and economics, pointing to worship as life in the real world as local and global followers of Jesus. Production and censorship is also important. Slow worship should be honest; rather than cover over our differences it should allow them to come out.

Reconciled unity is only meaningful if we bring our difference to the heart of the liturgy. This means you may not like what is going on in worship any given week but you have the opportunity and perhaps more importantly the spiritual responsibility to produce otherwise next week. In my experience our dominant worship culture rarely encourages or requires spiritual responsibility or gives people spiritual authority. Some of our favourite prayers from Credo were written by unlikely people. Homeless 'worship curators' who get the 'Son of Man had nowhere to lay his head' better than those of us with mortgages! Emerging worship isn't about video loops and candles or art, it's about worship that is authentically for the people, by the people and of the people.

As an activist missional 'mob' it is ultimately about a slow church movement. Slow food and Sabbath are profoundly connected. At 'Seeds Gatherings' for worship we don't expect anyone to attend anything or do anything and celebrate when people choose Sabbath rest over showing up on Sunday. Upon reading this my colleague Kate Allen questioned whether any church could really celebrate the non-attendance of its participants. Of course you want people committed to worshiping together, however this approach helps to emphasise that the 'Sunday Worship' event is only one element of a shared life which offers many resources to the wider community.

Our guiding principles push us to see our sense of community in the broadest terms. It can be those connected by geography, interest, the internet, occasional attendance, attendance at specific resourcing events and so on. However there is something countercultural about committing to a geography and a people that needs to be reclaimed.

Part of the vision for Seeds is that we develop cluster communities, small groups of committed people in different places bonded of covenanted to the disciplines that have made Seeds what it is:

- Discerning what is 'The Word' on the street.
- Growing home and sharing slow food.
- Re-imagining what Jesus' missionary instructions of healing, teaching and casting out evil might look like today.

The charism of Seeds seeks to encourage people to follow Jesus with the whole of their lives and be consumed not by 'church' activities but by an integrated sense of the mission of God in the world. Seedy mobs are missionaries who understand their community, their congregation, and what they are trying to achieve in their worship in any specific place and time: offering a fast food world a healthy taste of slow food, slow worship and slow church.

Some 'Seedy' prayers and blessings

We believe you know a group by their liturgy and prayers, so we have included some of our Seedy sayings.

Seeds Prayer of Promise

(Based upon the Seeds Covenant)

God our holy community of gracious hospitality, in the midst of our homelessness you extend us an invitation to Grow Home.

Help us to be a people who grow a rich sense of home. Let us teach each other the danger of wealth and the freedom of economic sharing. May the poor always be with us. Teach us the power and beauty of our bodies; fidelity with your wild creativity and respect for the sacred connections of your Spirit and all creation. Teach us how to eat slow so that our eyes may be opened to your presence through the breaking of bread. Extend to us no privilege other than that of Christian equality, teaching us the art of mutual submission. Grant us wisdom to know what laws to break and courage to break them. Teach us how to give of ourselves with the same passion with which you lived and died.

Lord hear us.

All: Lord hear our prayer.

May we know the Word.

May we know the stories of a God who recreates a fallen world, not just ancient words on a page but the living Spirit of Christ among us. Teach us how to choose our stories and story our choices; how to spin a life giving yarn and to listen for your voice in silence, at Sabbath and in the songlines of the land. Teach us to meditate and pray so that we may experience your love and cling to hope in the midst of failure, suffering and adversity.

Lord hear us.
All: Lord hear our prayer.

May we Go Engage.
May we have the confidence to engage our troubled world. To speak truth to the powers and to each other. To name and cast out that which is evil in our world and within, through militant nonviolence. Teach us the arts of hospitality, mercy and forgiveness. May we know how to negotiate the streets and danger by learning every community safety trick; and having done this, when and how to risk it all for the sake of love. Teach us the good work of love as the only true measure of success. And because each of us will fail, in the midst of our brokenness, may we know and share your healing power; your gracious hospitality to us.
Lord hear us.
All: Lord hear our prayer.

Seeds Lord's Prayer

Abba (Creator and Sustainer of our Household)
Wholly Unbrandable
May your economy come,
May your way be sung on the sacred earth we know.
Sustain us this day in the simplicity of enough.
Reconcile our debts with your forgiveness as we seek reconciliation with our debtors.
And lead us through the wilderness, away from the seduction of our vocation.
That in the face of evil our life may be saved.
Amen.

A Seedy Incarnational Benediction

In the beginning was the Word and the Word was God

And the Word became flesh and dwelt tabernacled,
Pitched the tent,
Moved into the neighbourhood,
Hit the street,
Among us.

God became a body!

As we prepare to leave, I want you to be aware of your body:
Your butt sitting on the seat,
Your dinner sitting at the bottom of your gut,
Your mind full of the many thoughts of this day.
You too are a body!
But you are more than just body.
More than 'consumer'.
More than your appetites and your urges.
May your body be charged, fired, infused with the power of the
Holy Spirit.
Like the saints of old may you be blessed with the knowledge
of the profound connection between flesh and spirit.
May you feel it in your body.
May you feel this connection when you eat.
May it be impossible for you to read the gospels without getting
hungry.
May you know what your food cost, not just what you paid for
it.
May it taste good!
May you feel this connection with the earth and all creation,
May your hands and feet get dirty.
May you grow some good fruit.
May you feel this connection with others.
May you love your neighbour, not the ones you wish you had
but the ones you do have; human and creature and creation!

May you be connected to community built on good sex and intimate friendships.
May you know peace and reconciliation in the war zones of relationship, family, household, church and culture.
You are the body of Christ!

Christ has no body here on earth but yours!
Christ has no hands but yours.
Christ has no feet but yours.
Christ has no butt but yours!
So get it up off your seat.
Dwell it, tabernacle it, pitch it, move it into the neighbourhood,
Hit the street with it.

And may God the Creator, Redeemer and Sustainer of all bodies go with you.
Amen.

The Community of Aidan and Hilda

The Community of Aidan and Hilda describes itself an international dispersed body of Christians who seek to cradle a Christian spirituality for today which renews the church and brings healing to fragmented people, communities and lands. It welcomes people of all backgrounds and countries who wish to be wholly available to God the Holy Trinity and to the way of Jesus as revealed to us in the Bible. The Community offers a Way of Life that is universal and for today. It draws inspiration from many sources, including desert and Celtic fathers and mothers. The Way of Life also calls us to be present to Christ in our own land and culture. For this reason followers of the Way of Life also look for sources of inspiration from within their own country.

Members follow a Way of Life, based on a rhythm of prayer

and study, simplicity, care for creation, and mission, seeking to weave together the separated strands of Christianity. Each shares their journey with a spiritual companion known as a soul friend. The Community aims to restore a holistic Christian spirituality reconnecting with the Spirit and the Scriptures, the saints and the streets, the seasons and the soil; to resource the emerging and existing church.

The work of the Community is the work of each member and can be expressed individually and corporately in many different ways including link cells and churches. Solidarity with other members is ultimately rooted in the knowledge that they follow the Community's Way of Life and that this reflects their deepest calling. However, they seek expressions of this in spiritual 'cradle places', such as England's Holy Island of Lindisfarne where members service a retreat house, chapel and study facility.

In common with many communities within Christianity, the Community has three vows. These are simplicity, purity and obedience which are understood as principles, not rules.

- *Simplicity* means we are willing to be rich or poor for God according to God's direction. We resist the temptation to be greedy or possessive, and we will not manipulate people or creation for our own ends. We are bold in using all we have for God without fear of possible poverty.

- *Purity* means we are wholehearted, not divided, in relationships. It means accepting and giving God our whole being, including our sexuality. We love all people as Christ commands, but the specific emotions and intimacy of sexual relations are expressed only in married life.

Some will be given a gift of marriage, some a gift of celibacy, and some will be given grace to continue a journey of not yet knowing. Each is to be equally respected and rejoiced in. We respect every person as belonging to God, and we are available to them with generosity and openness.

- *Obedience* is the joyful abandonment of ourselves to God. The root of obedience is attentive listening. We are most fulfilled when we foster a process of mutual discernment; this enables us to recognise that some people are charismatically or institutionally gifted in certain roles and we work with them to build up the common good. We respect each person and their role, and relate to them as an organ in a human body relates to every other organ (1 Corinthians 12).

Each member of this Community will have a soul friend to work with them in developing a Way of life that is personally suited to them. The Way relates to the following ten areas of life, and is reviewed at agreed intervals.

Life-long learning
Daily Bible reading is at the heart of this way of life. In addition, we study the history of the Celtic Church, becoming familiar with such saints as Aidan, Brigid, Caedmon, Columba, Cuthbert, David, Hilda, Illtyd, Ninian, Oswald and Patrick. We remember their feast days and consider them as companions on our journey of faith. We also bear in mind their strong link with the Desert Fathers and the Eastern Church, and wish to draw them and other sources into our field of studies. It is essential

that study is not merely as an academic exercise. All that we learn is not for the sake of study itself, but in order that what we learn should be lived. We encourage the Celtic practice of memorising Scriptures, and learning through the use of creative arts.

Spiritual journey

A soul friend is a friend with whom we openly share our spiritual journey. We meet with our soul friend at least twice a year. (S)he is someone a seeks to discern with us where we are on that journey, what the Spirit is doing in our lives, and how God is leading us. The soul friend respects the tradition that we come from. Thus, for example, some will seek a soul friend who is familiar with formal confession and penance. The soul friend gives guidance on two disciplines which the Community considers to be important:

Regular retreats

The outworking of this depends on the individual's own lifestyle, but we encourage regular days of quiet and reflection, and also an annual retreat.

Pilgrimage

The purpose of pilgrimage is to tread in the shoes of Christ or his saints in order to make contact with the many rich experiences which are to do with being a pilgrim. Such pilgrimages draw us into deeper devotion to our Lord Jesus and will inspire us to mission. Members might seek out communities of prayer. The Community recommends pilgrimage to sites of the Celtic Christian tradition, such as Iona and Lindisfarne as well as to new 'places of resurrection'. Soul friends give guidance about different ways of making pilgrimage.

Rhythm of prayer, work and re-creation

Prayer

We commit ourselves to a regular discipline of prayer. If required, our soul friend can give us guidance about this. The Community recommends the use of daily patterns of worship. The St Aidan Trust provides patterns of worship which are suited to the Way.

Ways of praying will vary according to temperament. The Community encourages a renewal of 'all kinds of praying' (Ephesians 6:18), and we are therefore committed to discovering new ways of praying, from contemplative prayer to celebratory praise.

Work

We welcome work as a gift from God. Every member should engage in work, whether it be the routine activities of life or paid employment. Work motivated by values which conflict with the Way should be avoided as much as possible. In humility we accept what God gives us. If we have no employment and are not clear what our work is, then we seek the advice of our soul friend. We seek not to overwork, standing firm against all pressure to do so, because it robs ourselves, others or God of the time we should give to them.

Rest

The hours of rest and recreation are as valuable as the hours of prayer and work. The Lord Jesus reminds us that 'the Sabbath was made for humankind, and not humankind for the Sabbath' (Mark 2:27). In the Scriptures even the land was given a Sabbath in the seventh year (Leviticus 25:3–5). The need for rest was built into creation (Genesis 2:1–3). A provision for this kind of rest, which is both holy and creative, should be part of each member's personal Way of Life.

Spiritual initiatives through intercession

The Community affirms a worldview that recognises the reality of the supernatural and of spiritual warfare. As Cuthbert and others 'stormed the gates of heaven', so we also need to engage in and to become familiar with intercessory prayer. We do not project on to the supernatural what belongs to the sphere of human responsibility. We affirm national initiatives in intercessory prayer.

Simplicity of lifestyle
We wish to 'live simply that others may simply live', to avoid any sense of judging one another; and God will make different demands of each of us. Our common responsibility is to regularly hold before God (and as appropriate to share with our soul friend) our income, our savings, our possessions, conscious that we are stewards, not possessors of these things, and making them available to him as he requires.

A simple lifestyle means setting everything in the simple beauty of creation. Our belongings, activities and relationships are ordered in a way that liberates the spirit; we cut out those things that overload or clutter the spirit.

We are not seeking a life of denial for we thoroughly rejoice in the good things God gives us. Our clothes and furniture should reflect God-given features of our personalities. There is a time to feast and celebrate as well as to fast. Our commitment is to openness. We stand against the influence of the god of mammon in our society by our life-style, by our hospitality, by our intercession, and by regular and generous giving.

Care for creation
We affirm God's creation as essentially good, but spoilt by the effects of human sin and satanic evil. We therefore respect nature and are committed to seeing it cared for and restored.

We aim to be ecologically aware, to pray for God's creation and all his creatures, and to stand against all that would seek to violate or destroy them. We look upon creation as a sacrament, reflecting the glory of God, and seek to meet God through his creation, to bless it, and to celebrate it.

Healing fragmented people and communities

We renounce the spirit of self-sufficient autonomy, and are committed to a much more holistic approach which was the strength of the Celtic church. We encourage the ministry of Christian healing. We not only lay hands on the sick and pray for their healing, we also 'lay hands' on every part of God's world to bless it and recognise its right to wholeness in Christ. We seek to become more fully human as we grow in Christ, and we believe that 'the glory of God is seen through a life fully lived' (Irenaeus).

Openness to God's Spirit

We allow God to take us where the Spirit wills, whether by gentle breeze or wild wind. The Celtic Christians had such faith in the leading of the Spirit that they gladly put to sea in small coracles, and went where the wind took them. We desire this kind of openness to the leading of the Spirit.

Essential to this is a proper affirmation of the gift of prophecy. St Paul urges us all to prophesy (1 Corinthians 14:1). We honour this gift and encourage its proper and appropriate use.

Learning to listen is a skill that has almost been lost, and which takes many years to acquire. We seek to cultivate an interior silence that recognises and sets aside discordant voices, to respond to unexpected or disturbing promptings of God, to widen our horizons, to develop 'the eye of the eagle' and see and hear God through his creation.

Unity

As we study the history of the Celtic church we discover the unity we once had as one Christian people within the one universal church. We are constantly ashamed of our divisions, and we repent of the schisms that have occurred from the Reformation onwards. We look upon all fellow Christians not as 'strangers but pilgrims together', and we honour those in oversight in all churches, not talking about our own denomination or others. We resist in our own lives things that damage the unity of Christ's body, and will not do separately what is best done together.

The Celtic church was thoroughly indigenous to the people in a way that the church has never been since. Aidan lived alongside the people and refused to accept the practices and customs that would distance him from the people and make him seem superior. The Celtic church honoured, trusted and went with the grain of the human communities it worked amongst. We seek to cultivate a solidarity with all people in everything except sin, to value all that is truly human in them, and to shed attitudes and practices that put up barriers between the church and the people.

We desire the healing of peoples divided by class, colour or creed and repent of our own part in these divisions.

Mission

Our aim is that 'the whole created order may be reconciled to God through Christ' (Colossians 1:20). We seek to live as one Christian community so 'that the world may believe' (John 17:21). The goal of the way of life is to develop a disciplined spirituality that will make us effective in our witness to Christ in the world.

The Celtic church evangelised from grassroots communities such as Lindisfarne, Iona and St David's. Our evangelism springs naturally from the community of our local church, and out of this Community. Bishops like Chad and Cedd were irrepressible evangelists as they travelled around. As we live out this life, the Holy Spirit leads us into new initiatives to bring God to the people. These will usually be through our churches at local or wider Community to pray, study and accomplish a particular God-given task.

We seek to share our faith wherever opportunity is given. We evangelise not simply out of a sense of duty, but because the Spirit of God is giving us a heart for the lost. We ask God to work through us in signs and wonders for his glory, not ours.

Our mission also includes speaking out for the poor, the powerless and those unjustly treated in our society, and to minister to and with them as God directs.

Chapter 6

New Monasticism

The second millennium church was based on order, and feared letting its members 'go with the flow'. Chaos theory in science reveals, however, a creative interaction between fluid particles, which become life-enhancing. The emerging church seeks flexible frameworks which enable all people to move and grow and flow with God's Spirit within the natural patterns around them.

There is a groundswell of Christians who put their energies into groups or networks rather than into congregations. While church attendance declines, Christian initiatives increase. The phrase *Liquid Church* has been used to describe this, as in Pete Ward's book of this title (Paternoster Press, 2002).

But how can these avoid being unreal, non-holistic, and like the over individualistic people in Moses' day, when everyone 'did what was right in their own eyes'? Christians who follow an individual path which keeps them on the move, uninvolved in the day-to-day life of a church, are like scattered fragments of metal—they need a magnet that can make them part of a pattern. They are like spokes not yet placed in a wheel—they need a hub to which they can relate. So also do many small churches. They don't respond to being slotted in to some bureaucratic arrangement; they need an organic relationship with a spiritual home.

So large numbers of Christian groups, networks, small churches, as well as mobile Christians outside them, cannot flourish unless there are also centres of stability, prayer, resource and hospitality to which they may relate.

We need more than celebration networks
In the 1980s the concept of cell-congregation-celebration developed. The celebration was the occasional coming together of congregations, and was probably arranged by the head-quarters of the umbrella network. This was not holistic. Sometimes congregations felt used.

We need more than umbrella churches
In the same period certain large, lively churches planted and nurtured new churches, and offered resources to them. Struggling or small congregations began to relate to them as umbrella churches. Churches such as Holy Trinity Brompton provide training days, faith-sharing teams, courses and consultancies. For these things they should be blessed. If umbrella churches are to become holistic hubs, however, they need to address how to provide an experience of lived community, unprogrammed space, daily corporate rhythm, and guest accommodation. Faith communities of other religions are ahead of the game in that they already have these.

We need more than multi-resource centres
Some churches have turned their buildings into multi-resource centres. Ann Morisy has some excellent insights into this in her book *Journeying Out: A New Approach to Christian Mission* (Continuum, 2006). She says that a number of churches have spent money on making their buildings user friendly for the wider community. However she says that:

> For those outside the church the mundane
> symbols associated with a community building
> can easily dominate their perceptions. The vast
> majority of people who are not involved in
> church life will probably look upon the newly
> created church centre within the church building
> as indicative of it retreating from its former
> capacity . . . Rather than communicating rele-
> vance and hospitality, the community facilities
> can easily communicate has given up and quit
> the scene . . .[44]

Morisy goes on to say that we need to find a balance in finding
the place for the sacred in the places we make public.

The new monasticism

An increasing number of Christians are turning to 'the new
monasticism'. Dietrich Bonhoeffer wrote in a prophetic letter to
his brother Karl in January 1935:

> The restoration of the Church must surely come
> from a new kind of monasticism, which will have
> only one thing in common with the old, a life
> lived without compromise according to the
> Sermon on the Mount in the following of Jesus. I
> believe the time has come to gather people
> together for this.[45]

Because of his execution in a prison cell shortly before the end
of World War II we shall never know how he would have
developed a new monasticism. Sadly, the German Church did
not take hold of what he had conceived. In Scotland, however,
George McLeod had been developing the Iona Community

during those same war years. Bonhoeffer's *Life Together* became standard reading there.

A generation after Bonhoeffer the evangelical leader John Stott called for 'the re-monking' of the church. In this decade Eugene Petersen has called on Protestant church leaders to replace their 'ego lust to be god' with a corporate pattern that makes space for God:

> Historically the most conspicuous corporate construction that does this is the monastery . . . The genius of the monastery is its comprehensiveness; all the hours of the day are defined by prayer; all the activity of the monks is understood as prayer . . . This external comprehensiveness penetrates community and soul.

He quotes Oxford historian Herbert Butterfield, who wrote 'Sometimes I wonder at dead of night whether, during the next fifty years, Protestantism may not be at a disadvantage because a few centuries ago, it decided to get rid of monks.' Petersen calls for 'an open monastery', and concludes:

> What is critical is an imagination large enough to contain all of life, all worship and work in prayer set in a structure adequate to the actual conditions in which it is lived out.[46]

In the Catholic tradition, or more broadly the Western church, there is a notion of 'Mendicant Orders' and 'Monastic Orders'. Mendicant orders are commonly known as 'Apostolic Religious Orders'. These orders are more committed to action and not necessarily tied to geography. This is in contrast to 'monastic orders' where monks are committed to a life of contemplation in a specific geography or monastery and were defined as enclosed communities. Both orders have elements of both the apostolic and the contemplative; however a real synthesis of each model is needed. This is evident in the Celtic tradition.

The new monasticism transcends both the Protestant and Roman Catholic monastic frameworks which have dominated the Western church since the Reformation. It is a discernment of shared rhythms; it is a recovery of normality. Some of the churches arising out of the sixteenth-century Protestant-Catholic schism have been dogmatically separatist. They have seen themselves as the centre of reform and have tended to look down on others. Monasticism, in contrast, is grounded in a humility that has no grandiose illusions. It has a deep connectedness which derives from a recognition that there is only one holy, catholic, orthodox, apostolic church.

Postmodern Christians who seek a new monasticism are wary of structures that are imposed from the centre; they do not want to be trapped in a new legalism; they don't want to be shut off from ordinary people. They see themselves as on a journey, and can't prejudge what they will be doing at a later stage of the journey. They want to be free to follow each prompting of the Spirit, to be single or to marry. Nevertheless, those who embrace new monasticism seek to be connected to the Self-Emptying God in the centre and in the streets, in the other parts of the Body of Christ and in their own hearts.

Planting people-friendly monastic communities that are born out of such a dynamic, and which do not have to be squeezed into a 'one shape fits all' church structure, may be the only way to win people. For monasteries, whether old or new, are usually freed from the diocesan system so that they can develop under God according to their own prophetic charisms. This is recognised, in one way or another, in the regulations of the historic diocesan churches.[47]

The Cappadocian and other fathers of the Eastern Church did not treat fourth century monasticism as a special form of Christian life, but as an actualisation of what in principle was a life demanded of all Christians.[48] The Celtic monastic churches were not regarded as a special form of church, they were the norm, for everybody could belong to them.

A lot of work and thought is happening around new monasticism in the US. It's coming from years of solid foundations from Dorothy Day and others like her. A book edited by the Rutba House, called *School(s) for Conversion: 12 Marks of a New Monasticism* (Cascade Books), identifies these marks:

- Relocation to abandoned places of empire.
- Sharing economic resources with fellow community members and the needy among us.
- Hospitality to the stranger.
- Lament for racial divisions and active pursuit of a just reconciliation.
- Humble submission to Christ's Body, the church.
- Intentional formation and a community rule.
- Nurturing common life amongst members of intentional community.
- Support for celibates, married couples and children.
- Geographical proximity to community members.
- Care for the plot of God's Earth given to us and supporting our local economies.
- Peacemaking in the midst of violence and conflict resolution.
- Commitment to a disciplined contemplative life.[49]

The Lindisfarne Community in New York describes New Monasticism as follows:

> The monastic way was always a demanding and disciplined life. It required leaving home and family to live with others who shared the Rule. The new monasticism will, likewise, be demanding, but in different ways. Most in the new monasticism will not live in enclosed communities or commit themselves to a wandering life of preaching and poverty. The new monastics will come from a variety of walks of life and most will not be committed to celibacy. They will seek to engage in the practices of prayer, meditation, study and service in the midst of busy family and work lives. Theirs will be a radical discipleship in finding Christ in the very heart of twenty-first century life—the breaking down of sacred and secular.[50]

Can existing churches be monastic?

We have seen that in early Christian Ireland many of the churches were monastic communities. In the Eastern Orthodox Church a bond between parish and monastery has often been retained. In the West, however, churches are generally thought of as having nothing to do with monasteries. There are some exceptions. A modern example of a monastery that is also an Episcopal Church is The Community of Jesus, Orleans. This began in 1958 with two women offering a ministry of teaching, prayer and charismatic renewal. This attracted a small group of people to move to these grounds on the shores of Cape Cod Bay. They covenanted to live together in mutual service and honesty. Several families soon followed, to share in the common life of prayer and work.

In 1970, the Community of Jesus was formally constituted. For more than thirty years, the Community's pattern of life has evolved in the Benedictine spirit and is summarised in its own Rule of Life. Today there are approximately 165 professed members, and fifty children and young people who live in privately owned homes that surround the church and guest house. The celibate brothers and sisters live in their respective houses—the Friary and the Convent. Each of the Community households consists of more than one family, often with several generations represented, who share together in the daily tasks of home-life. Household families and individuals are financially responsible for themselves, while also committed to care for one another's needs <www.communityofjesus.org>.

Monasteries can be churches, but at first sight it seems unlikely that churches can become monasteries. One reason is that leaders of churches are appointed by bishops or boards with a non-monastic agenda. In religious communities, in contrast, the spiritual leader evolves from within in an organic relationship of unconditional commitment. A second reason is that in monasteries the core members commit to be available for certain duties and to live by values for which they are held accountable. Church members are not required to make such commitments. A third reason is that churches employ staff with pay differentials; in monasteries everyone is equal.

Although it seems unlikely that churches can become monasteries, changes in society require churches to adapt in ways that have more in common with Celtic monastic churches than with Sunday only congregations. For example:

- A twenty-four-hour society calls for seven-day-a-week churches.
- A cafe society calls for churches that are eating places.
- A travelling society calls for churches that provided accommodation.
- A stressed society calls for churches that provide spaces for silence and retreat.
- A multi-choice society calls for churches that have a choice of styles and facilities.

So it may be worthwhile looking at trends and possibilities in the emerging church which recover something of a monastic spirit or framework.

Existing churches that are restoring certain monastic features

A growing number of churches provide daily public prayer, cafes, conference facilities or work projects. Such churches are listed on the Community of Aidan and Hilda web site <www.aidanandhilda.org>. The Church of the Saviour, Washington, has some ten congregations each with a distinct project in different locations such as cafe, drugs rehab centre, old people's circle, study centre. Membership entails a year's discipleship course, the writing of a personal spiritual profile, and a covenant. A small group maintain daily prayer in a central location.

Mega churches

In the USA two million people belong to mega churches. These contain certain elements of the Celtic monastic city. The mega church has food halls, sporting leagues, day care and learning groups as well as a variety of worship patterns. 'I am not the pastor of a church, I am the mayor of a city', observed the leader of one mega church. The mega churches lack, however, the spirituality of the monastic tradition, they do not pray daily in the rhythms of creation, or adopt common spiritual disciplines.

In Bergen, Norway, the 2,400-member Pentecostal Church also has certain elements of the monastic village. It has schools for children and adults and is starting its own bank. Every day over a hundred people gather for an hour's prayer meeting before going to work. But without cars this would disintegrate. Nobody lives there. It is not a spiritual home. Its members are living off a society which is dysfunctional; they are not creating an alternative economy.

Villages of God

A new university opened before it had finished landscaping, so the planners observed where the students planted their footprints and laid the paths there. Is that a parable for the emerging church? Many Christians and spiritual seekers today make their way towards the fast reviving pilgrim centres, the growing dispersed communities, umbrella churches or yearly gatherings. The common factor is the search for some kind of spiritual home.

I believe that these developments, combined with the fresh shoots we have considered, point to the potential emergence of what I term 'villages of God'. The mushrooming of Christian projects, culture-friendly church plants and networks alongside the decline in the 'one-shape-fits-all' type of church make possible patterns that are more flexible than the old, which, when the place and time are right, can cohere around some common values, facilities and rhythms. By imaginatively linking these new networks with traditional churches the marginalised parts can become part of the whole.

Although village isn't a word often used in Australia, international airports and shopping centres increasingly feature villages, and I think it captures a sense of community and geography. These villages start where people are. Some grow piecemeal. Others grow as a result of congregations and networks planning how to creatively link together. Some which seem disparate to the eye, show up as something like a village on a web site provided by the churches and projects of an area.

This is not a return of the Christendom model. These villages of God serve; they do not oust the institutions that exist in the area. These villages of God are resonant of the early Celtic monastery model of church. The following diagram illustrates the concept.

Certain 'villages' will be in one geographical area, others will be more dispersed but their various parts can be linked by pilgrim trails and web sites. They are open to everyone. They serve and build good relationships with the people, forge a deep and prayerful relationship which transforms localities. A village of God could consist, for example, of a Salvation Army Soup Kitchen, a Roman Catholic Oratory, an Anglican daily worship centre, a Uniting Church day centre a Pentecostal youth congregation, a charitable social project and entrepreneurial workshops. Many Celtic monastic churches had a real economy which was viable, rooted in the neighbourhood and seen to benefit local people. It is, I believe, possible for us to reconnect with these roots and develop monastic villages on a smaller, more organic scale.

Seven day-a-week emerging villages of God typically include daily corporate prayer. They might have more than one style of worship area, a cafe, an arts centre, workshops, guest accommodation, study and sports facilities, shops, play groups, play area, a theatre or meeting hall, counselling and medical care, huts for private study and contemplation, schools, support groups for needy families, the homeless, addicts, activities for the elderly, meditation rooms, organic fields or farm, peace garden and cyber facilities, all revolving around a daily rhythm of prayer, and a place of silence serviced by resident members who embrace common values and disciplines.

Pilgrim centres such as Iona, Lindisfarne and Taize have elements of 'the monastic village' and draw many seekers. However, unlike the early monastic villages, whose various components grew out of the common wellspring of God's love, these places already have indigenous sub-communities, such as fishing, farming and tourism, with their own dynamics; the 'godly village' approach must be to respect these as they are, not to duplicate them, though holding out the possibility of voluntary transformation.

The values of villages of God

Churches in villages of God acknowledge that the part is not the whole. The villages enable churches to be true to themselves and more sustaining of their society. In villages of God the prayer oratory of one tradition or the soup kitchen of another can be true to its root—but each can flower because it is in an environment that does not attack it.

Villages of God become prejudice-free, hate-free, fear-free, earth-friendly fair trade zones. These villages offer the soil of reflection and the wisdom of the forgiving heart. They foster that love which inspires inner transformation, stable relationships, and motivation to live healthy, law abiding, earth-cherishing lives.

Epilogue

Lands of the Eternal Spirit

Early European explorers searched for *'terra australis incognito'* (the unknown south land) believing that there would be great riches on this mysterious continent. As far as we know, the first explorer to discover and name this land was the Spanish sailor Pedro Fernandez de Quiros. On the Day of Pentecost, 14 May 1606, he wrote: 'Let the heavens, the earth and waters witness that in the name of Jesus Christ I hoist this emblem of the holy cross . . . on this part of the south . . . which from now on shall be called the southern land of the Holy Spirit'. Was this prophetic? Many Christians believe this reflected something of the eternal designs of God that transcended the cultural confines of the man who spoke it.

The Lord spoke to Moses face to face as one speaks to a friend . . . and said: 'My presence will go with you' (Exodus 33:11). In this way Moses' people became distinct. As people in Australia and New Zealand come deeply into God's presence their people will become God's in distinctive ways.

Moses' people had to be stripped of inessentials and impediments. Those who hardened their hearts never made it. God is calling Australians and New Zealanders to strip away imported, unnecessary impedimenta.

Moses met God through creation (first a bush, then clouds by day and by night). God is calling Australians and New Zealanders to become fully present to Him in their soil, sea and sky.

God took Moses up into the darkness of a mountain. God is calling Australians to embrace their shadow.

As they respond God will say of these two lands, as once God said of Israel: 'Are you my dear child? The child I delight in? I am deeply moved for you. I will surely have mercy on you' (Jeremiah 31:20).

The Southern Cross and the circle

Those who make promises to follow the Aidan and Hilda Way of Life wear a wooden cross with a circle. This represents the integration of primal realities with God's all-embracing mercy. Christ's sacrifice was intended to transform the whole of creation and the whole of life.

Following the 1967 referendum which voted in favour of Aboriginal people having citizens' rights, certain Aboriginal leaders produced a black, red and yellow Aboriginal flag. The black represents the Aboriginal people, the red represents the earth, and the yellow circle represents the sun, the unifying factor that gives life to all. This was hoisted on National Aboriginal Day, 12 July 1971, and again at the 1972 'Tent Embassy' in Canberra. It represents a powerful and uniting symbol of identity for Aboriginal people and a growing number of others throughout Australia.

The circle is a primal symbol that embraces all creatures and all people. In a quite different way the circle of the sun has been a unifying factor for settler Australians: it has produced a sunny disposition, an enjoyment of the outdoors and an out-going attitude.

The cross is a universal symbol that speaks of forgiveness, hope and life rising from the ashes of wrongs and weakness. The official flag of Australia contains the cross. This is currently in the form of the British union flag and also the Southern Cross star formation. Many Australians wish that, if there were to be a republic, an Indigenous form of flag could be imagined that embraces these insights.

The sun circle surely has a place in any new all-Australian flag. The cross is a universal symbol that speaks of forgiveness, hope and life rising from the ashes of wrongs and weakness. The southern star locates the region.

A Western-Eastern church?

Australia has already decided to embrace the East economically, hence its membership of APEC (Asia Pacific Economic Cooperation). Recent Anzac governments have hesitated to embrace the lands to the east of them politically, but church and other people have invested much effort and money in projects such as the tsunami relief in Indonesia.

The world needs to know that Christianity is an Eastern as much as it is a Western religion. One way the emerging Anzac church can embrace the East is to incorporate rituals, ikons and prayer practices from the Eastern Orthodox and Oriental Churches, as does the Breakwater Community. The Anzac church can become indigenous as it embraces the shadow of the people who now live in these lands, whatever their ancestry.

The Community of Aidan and Hilda in Australia and New Zealand

> Make guideposts. Consider the road by which you travelled. How long will you waver? Return to your Source.
>
> Jeremiah 31:21

We are an international movement of people who seek to restore Christianity as a way of life, and to earth this in a way that is indigenous to each land. We seek to weave together God-given strands in Christianity which have become separated. We believe Australia has an opportunity to pattern a Christianity which weaves together Eastern and Western strands and offer hope to the world.

We will live a rhythm of prayer and action, mind and body, justice and simplicity.

We will apply the 'can-do' attitude of 'the Battlers' to spiritual as well as physical dimensions of life.

We will practice awareness of God in the elements.

We will stand with the poor of the world.

We will heal the land and speak truth to power—all in the love of Christ.

Anzacs cannot connect with particular places in the way Aboriginal peoples did: but we can embrace our connectedness.

We cannot have their dreams: but we can learn to dream.

We cannot act as if mental processes have remained unchanged: but when there are silences we can enter into and not abort them

We will rise up days of light

I arise today in the wisdom of the One who brought to birth the giant plains, the water and the first beings.
I arise today in the brightness of the One who created the blazing sun, the shining stars and the twinkle in our eyes.

We will rise up in days of dark

I arise today in the Eternal Flow of Mercy who was here when the land began to breathe, when the first tribes began to roam, and when the colonists came to settle.
I arise today in the Eternal Flow of Wisdom who is dimly perceived in the stones, the stories and the studies of the people.

I arise today in the Eternal Flow of Life who seeps through
land, and limb and love.
We will say sorry for past blindness
Sometimes we take earth for granted.

For this we are sorry.

Sometimes we take those who were before us for granted.

For this we are sorry.

Sometime we take those who have come after us for granted.

For this we are sorry.

We will declare our faith:

You are a God who hurts when we hurt others.
You are a God who does not hold this against us.
You are a God who teaches us when we reap what we sow.
You are a God who shares our life.

We will pray:

Christ of this Island Continent,
Let us this morning not be frightened,
By the feel of your energetic presence,
But rather courageous, strong and hopeful.
Christ of Change and Movement,
Let us glimpse you,
In the terrifying terrains of the soul,
Where you seem to be absent and cruel.
Christ of Justice,

Let us be patient,
When our institutions fail us,
Or we are affected by other's fear and hatred.
Christ of Waiting,
Let us wait for wisdom,
To draw us into the Intimate,
Christ Heart of this land.
Christ of brokenness,
Let us be held,
In the bosom of our waters, deserts, mountains and bushlands,
Always searching for beauty in the midst of chaos and despair.
Amen.

> Matthew Lamont from his *Australian Prayer Rhythms*

We will commune

Also in my own birth's story
Let me see God's love and glory.

In rhythms of the earth I see
Your order and a peace for me.

Every plant and bird and tree
Can be your love letter to me.

Loved by people and the land
I'm standing tall in God's hand.

As the water in the stream
Makes its journey to the sea
So through troubles I will flow
To the God I truly know.

> John Hunt of Christchurch, New Zealand

We will covenant

Today, we make a covenant with this land.

As a branch is grafted onto a mature stock,

So we want to be grafted onto the ancient heritage of this land,

So that its life may flow through us.

We commit ourselves to the land we live in and to all who belong to it,

Most particularly our Indigenous people

And also the newcomers to this country,

Who have bound themselves to this land.

We will care for it with gentleness, patience, simplicity and compassion,

Rather then merely something to be bought and sold.

We will see the land as a gift for which we are truly thankful,

And undertake the privileged duty of respecting and looking after it.

We thank God, the Great Creator Spirit, for all the earth provides:

Water, food, and all the riches above and below the ground.

We undertake to use them sparingly and thoughtfully.

As we enter more deeply into the Spirit of the land,

We see the land as a Sacrament and Icon of our mothering Creator Spirit.

Be still.

Listen to the breath of the Spirit which has blown through it for ages past,

Today, and always;

For this is: The Spirit of the Dreaming.

Amen.

Catholic Social Justice Council[51]

We will grow
God help us
To rise up from our struggle.
Like a tree rises up from the soil.
Our roots reaching down to our trouble.
Our rich, dark dirt of existence.
Finding nourishment deeply
And holding us firmly.
Always connected.
Growing upwards and into the sun.
Amen.
                Michael Leunig[52]

Postscript
The need for reconciliation, and the need for the word sorry to be used, is picked up a number of times throughout this book. Our new Prime Minister Kevin Rudd has just officially apologised to the stolen generations as this book is going to print. I write this postscript having just returned from Federation Square where I watched a live screening from Parliament House in Canberra of this momentous occasion.

Rudd's speech was heartfelt and statesman-like as well as entirely personal.

'For the pain, suffering and hurt of these Stolen Generations, their descendants and for their families left behind, we say sorry.

To the mothers and the fathers, the brothers and the sisters, for the breaking up of families and communities, we say sorry.

And for the indignity and degradation thus inflicted on a proud people and a proud culture, we say sorry.'

Like many around me, I felt tears welling up as these words were finally uttered after more than a decade of silence under the Howard Government. As the applause rang out at the end of Rudd's speech, my wife commented to me that you could almost hear it reverberating throughout history.

The most powerful moment for me, however, occurred as I was leaving Federation Square just after Rudd's speech. Cutting back through St Paul's Cathedral on my way to Collins Street, I bumped in to an indigenous guy that I knew from the streets. I wished him a happy sorry day and we embraced. We then turned and looked over the crowd at Federation Square from our vantage point. You could just make out the opposition leader Brendan Nelson on the big screen in the distance (who was later criticised for his speech).

Amazed by the size of the crowd, my indigenous friend remarked, 'You white fellas must want this as much as us black fellas'.

'I think you're right,' I responded.

'My mum would have loved this.' He hesitated, then said, 'I think I want to cry'.

'So do I.'

We stood in silence for a few moments, looking over the crowd at Federation Square, in silence for a few minutes.

We embraced again. As I walked away I felt a deep sense of hope for our nation.

Brent Lyons Lee
February 13, 2008

End Notes

1. David Tacey, *Re-enchantment: A New Australian Spirituality* (Harper Collins, 2000), 97.
2. Tacey, *op cit,* 139.
3. Tacey, *op cit,* 99–100.
4. Tim Costello, *Tips From a Traveling Soul-Searcher* (Allen & Unwin, 1999), 6.
5. CJ Jung, *A Psychological Approach to the Dogma of the Trinity* (Collected Works, Volume 11) para 267.
6. Darren Cronshaw, *Credible Witness: Companions, Prophets, Hosts and Other Australian Mission Models* (UNOH, 2006), 20.
7. David B Barrett, editor, *World Christian Encyclopaedia: A Comparative Survey of Churches and Religions in the Modern World, AD 1900–2000* (Oxford University Press, 1982).
8. See, for example, in Grace Davie *Religion in Britain since 1945: Believing without Belonging* (Blackwell Publishers, 1994).
9. PL Berger, *Sacred Canopy* (Anchor Books, 1988).
10. Diarmuid O'Murchu, *Quantum Theology* (Crossroad 1997).
11. Leonardo Boff, *The Maternal Face of God: The Feminine and its Religious Expressions* (Collins, 1989).
12. Francis Fukuyama, *The Weekend Financial Times* (June 12–13 1999).
13. Thomas Berry, CP, with Thomas Clarke, SJ, *Befriending the Earth* (Twenty Third Publications, 1991).
14. Ronald Ferguson, *George McLeod: Founder of the Iona Community* (William Collins, 1990), 108.
15. Frank McLynn , *Carl Gustav Jung* (St Martin's Press, 1997).
16. Gerald A Arbuckle, SM, *Out of Chaos: Refounding Religious Congregations* (Geoffrey Chapman, 1988).
17. Rick Joyner, 'The Twenty-First Century Church' from *Prophetic Bulletin* (Morning Star Publications, September 1999).
18. Robert Warren, *Being Human: Being Church* (Marshall Pickering, 1995).

19. Mark Stibbe, *O Brave New Church* (Darton, Longman & Todd, 1995).
20. Tom Wright, *New Tasks for a Renewed Church* (Hodder & Stoughton, 1992).
21. Michael Riddell, *Threshold of the Future: Reforming the Church in the Post-Christian West* (SPCK, 1998).
22. The Life of Gildas was probably written by a monk at the monastery of Rhuys, Brittany in the ninth century. See *Two Lives of Gildas*, translated by Hugh Williams (Llanerch, 1990).
23. Paul Cavill, *Anglo-Saxon Christianity* (Fount, 1999) explores this, though rather uncritically.
24. Christine Fell, *Women in Anglo Saxon England and the Impact of 1066* (British Museum Publications, 1984).
25. George Hunter, *The Celtic Way of Evangelism* (Abingdon Press, 1999).
26. John Finney, *Recovering the Past: Celtic and Roman Mission* (Darton, Longman &Todd, 1996).
27. *The Celtic Prayer Book*, Volume Three, *Healing the Land; Sacraments and Special Services* (Kevin Mayhew, 2003).
28. Federic Brussat, and Mary Ann, *Spiritual Literacy: Reading the Sacred in Everyday Life* (Simon & Schuster, 1998).
29. *Daily Telegraph*, 29 May 1999.
30. David J Bosch, *Transforming Mission: Paradigm Shifts in Theology of Mission* (Orbis Books, 1991).
31. George Hunter, *The Celtic Way of Evangelism* (Abingdon Press, 1999), 54.
32. Aylward Shorter, *Evangelism and Culture* (Chapman, 1994).
33. *The Plough*, October 1997.
34. D Hay, *Religious Experience Today* (Mowbray/Cassell, 1990).
35. R Nye and D Hay, 'Investigating Children's Spirituality: How Do You Start Without a Starting Point?' in *British Journal of Education* 18:3.
36. *Ibid*, 152.
37. Marie-Louise Sjoestedt, *Gods and Heroes of the Celts* (Turtle Island Foundation, 1982).

38. Notes supplied by John Smith from his seminary in USA.

39. Rowan Williams, *Ffydd ac Argyfwng Cenedl* (Faith and the Crisis of a Nation) volume 2 (John Penri Press, 1982).

40. Indian Bible Church, 595 South Logan Street, Denver, Colorado 80209 USA.

41. Roger Ellis and Chris Seaton, *New Celts* (Kingsway Publications, 1998).

42. Rob Frost, *Which Way for the Church?* (Kingsway Publications, 1996).

43. This is explored in Joyner, Rick, *Leadership, Management and the Five Essentials for Success* (Morning Star Publications, 1995).

44. Ann Morisy, *Journeying Out: A New Approach to Christian Mission* (Continuum, 2004), 184–5.

45. Quoted in Mary Bosanquet, *The Life and Death of Dietrich Bonhoeffer* (Hodder and Staughton, 1968), chapter 11.

46. Eugene Petersen, *The Belly of the Fish* (Eerdmans/Gracewing).

47. For example, The Advisory Council on the Relations of Bishops and Religious Communities in the Church of England states in A Directory of the Religious Life (1980): 'Religious communities are independent associations expressing by their life and work a prophetic role which complements, and sometimes challenges, the life of the church as a whole. They therefore need freedom from external control. Their status as independent bodies gives them complete and autonomous control of both their property and their internal government, in fulfilment of their spiritual vision. Yet the Church requires what both clergy and laity ask for: standards or norms by which religious communities can be guaranteed and recognised as in good standing.'

48. RA Greer, *Broken Lights and Mended Lives* (Pennsylvania State University Press, 1986).

49. Rutba House, *School(s) for Conversion: 12 Marks of a New Monasticism* (Cascade Books, 2005).

50. The Lindisfarne Community, New York, (www.icmi.org).

51. The covenant prayer is by Betty Pike from the Catholic Social Justice:
Website:www.socialjustice.catholic.org.au/Content/spirituality/spirituality_covenant_land.html
52. Michael Leunig, *The Prayer Tree* (CollinsDove, 1991).

Index

Aborigines, 5, 6, 7, 4, 13, 14, 15, 16, 138, 140

Aboriginal spirituality, 8, 13, 15

Allen, Kate, 110

Andrews, Dave and Angie, 103

Anglican Church, 6, 34

Arbuckle, Gerald, 29

Augustine, 44, 71

Australian spirituality, 6, 8

Baptist Churches, 6

Barr, Jim, 92

Barth, Karl, 70

Berger, Peter, 22

Berry, Thomas, 25

Bessell, Brad 3

Blake, William, 27

Boff, Leonardo, 23

Bonhoeffer, Dietrich, 125

Bosch, David, 66

Brett, Mark, 105

Butterfield, Herbert, 126

Cadbury, Adrian, 79 Cannon, Liz, 69

Capsanis, George, 53

Celtic Christians, 36, 39, 40, 50, 71, 121

Celtic church, 3, 39, 44, 80, 121, 122, 123

Celtic style, 42, 43, 44, 45, 82

Chapman, Peter, 93

Collins Street Baptist Church, 93, 94, 95

Columba, 4, 8, 36, 39, 41, 117

Community of Aidan and Hilda, 8, 3, 37, 54, 83, 115, 131, 138, 139

Costello, Tim, 8, 9, 92, 93, 94

Credo Café, 95, 96, 97, 105, 108

Cronshaw, Darren, 14

Curnow, Marcus, 100

Dalrymple, William, 19

Dearlove, Des, 79

Duckworth, Justin and Jenny, 85

Eastern Church, 118, 128, 139

Ellis, Roger, 75

Emerging Church, 4, 7, 8, 3, 7, 11, 12, 15, 22, 47, 52, 55, 65, 66, 71, 72, 74, 78, 81, 82, 123, 131, 132

Episcopal Church, 130

Finney, John, 50, 67

Frost, Rob, 75

Fukuyama, Francis, 24

Gandhi, 29

Goleman, Daniel, 80

Green, Laurie, 50

Griffiths, Bede, 22

Gunnerson, Denny, 74

Hague, William, 70

Haire, Kim Erickson, 72, 73

Ham, Ron, 92

Harland, Ian, 35

Harries, Richard, 22

Hay, David, 69

Hoffman, Virginia Curran, 6

Hooper, Catherine, 66

Hunter, George, 42, 67

Holy Transfiguration Community, 12

Hospitality, 54, 56, 128

Illich, Ivan, 9

Iona, 8, 4, 34, 36, 54, 59, 118,
123, 126, 135

Jewish, 47, 60, 61, 71

John Paul 11, 33

Jones, E Stanley, 29

Joyner, Rick, 32

Jung, CJ, 12, 13, 27, 47, 146

Knox, John, 26

Lacey, Chris, 97

Lamont, Matthew, 4, 142

Lindisfarne, 4, 7, 9, 4, 34, 37, 43,
65, 82, 116, 118, 123, 129,
135

Macleod, Fiona (William Sharpe)
58, 59

Manning, Kevin, 17

Maori, 88, 89, 90, 91

McLeod, George, 26, 126

Merton, Thomas, 77

Monastic churches, 9, 36, 41,
128, 131, 134

Monasticism, 6, 123, 125, 127,
128, 129

Mother Teresa, 29, 68

Morgan, Marlo, 14, 15

Maximus the Confessor, 71

Mega churches, 132

Miley, Caroline, 6

Millennium, 47, 75

Monasteries, 35, 36, 37, 81, 105,
126, 127, 130, 133

Morisy, Ann, 124

Muslim, 17, 33

National Sorry Days, 16

Nouwen, Henri, 62

Nye, Rebecca, 69

O'Murchu, Diarmuid. 23

Open Tables, 78

Orthodox, 9, 12, 49, 76, 83, 87,
130, 139

Pawson, David, 44

Petersen, Eugene, 126

Pierson, Mark, 99, 108

Potter, Philip, 51

Prayer, 8, 10, 17, 33, 35, 36, 37,
38, 40, 43, 44, 46, 51, 52, 53,

54, 61, 62, 63, 75, 76, 94,
108, 112, 113, 116, 118, 119,
120, 124, 126, 127, 129, 130,
131, 132, 134, 135, 139, 140
Price, Clive, 74
Prince Charles, 51
Rainbow Spirit Theology, 15
Reformation, 25, 26, 122, 127
Reformed churches, 42
Robinson, Martin and Alison, 83,
85
Roman Catholic Churches, 6

Seaton, Chris, 75
Second millennium church, 23,
123
Sine, Tom, 43
Siorain, Joe O, 43
Songlines, 101, 106, 112
St Aidan, 66, 119
St Benedict, 36, 81
St Cuthbert, 81
St Patrick, 35
Sumerians, 64
Sumner, John, 20, 28
Tacey, David, 3, 5, 7, 8, 146
Tavener, John, 49

Trad, Keysar, 17
Tutu, Desmond, 34

Urban Neighbours of Hope, 83
Urban Seed, 83, 92–106, 109–
112
Urban Vision, 83, 84, 85, 86, 88,
89, 92

Waiters Union, 83, 102
Wallace, Martin, 60, 66
Ward, Pete, 123
Warren, Robert, 32, 56, 59
Williams, Charles, 66
Williams, Rowan, 5, 74
Wimber, John, 80
Wood, Chorley, 32
World Vision Australia, 8

YFC, 85, 86, 87
Young, Nick and Phillippa, 85

Printed in the USA
CPSIA information can be obtained
at www.ICGtesting.com
JSHW022232170324
59187JS00003B/205